# MEDIA RESEARCH TECHNIQUES

Second Edition

# MEDIA
# RESEARCH
# TECHNIQUES

Second Edition

Arthur Asa Berger

SAGE Publications
*International Educational and Professional Publisher*
Thousand Oaks   London   New Delhi

*For information:*

SAGE Publications, Inc.
2455 Teller Road
Thousand Oaks, California 91320
E-mail: order@sagepub.com

SAGE Publications Ltd.
6 Bonhill Street
London EC2A 4PU
United Kingdom

SAGE Publications India Pvt. Ltd.
M-32 Market
Greater Kailash I
New Delhi 110 048 India

Printed in the United States of America

*Library of Congress Cataloging-in-Publication Data*

Berger, Arthur Asa, 1933-
    Media research techniques/by Arthur Asa Berger.—2nd ed.
        p.  cm.
    Includes bibliographical references (p.    ) and index.
    ISBN 0-7619-1536-2 (acid-free paper).—ISBN 0-7619-1537-0
(pbk.: acid-free paper)
    1. Mass media—Research—Methodology.  I. Title.
    P91.3.B386    1998
    302.23′072—dc21                                                    97-45406

98  99  00  01  02  03  04  10  9  8  7  6  5  4  3  2  1

| | |
|---|---|
| *Acquiring Editor:* | Margaret H. Seawell |
| *Editorial Assistant:* | Renée Piernot |
| *Production Editor:* | Astrid Virding |
| *Production Assistant:* | Denise Santoyo |
| *Typesetter/Designer:* | Marion Warren |
| *Cover Designer:* | Candice Harman |
| *Print Buyer:* | Anna Chin |

# Contents

## Part II. Writing and Thinking

# Preface

I wrote the first edition of *Media Research Techniques* because I thought it would be a good idea to enable students to try their hands at doing research themselves. I didn't want students to be limited only to studying what other researchers had done. It is valuable and important to learn about the history of media research, but I felt that was not enough. And most of the textbooks I looked at struck me as too theoretical; they didn't put much emphasis on having students actually do research.

So I designed a book that had a number of research projects that I thought students would find interesting and that they could do with minimum experience in a limited amount of time. In the years since the book was published, a number of colleagues and other scholars I've met at conferences have suggested that I add new chapters to the book. They have said things like, "If you had a chapter on experimentation I'd really be pleased" and "Why don't you add a chapter on historical research?" As a result of these comments, I have revised *Media Research Techniques.* My editor at Sage Publications, Margaret Seawell, asked a number of people who teach media research for their suggestions, and I've adopted a number of them in this second edition. I am grateful for the helpful comments of these scholars, and for their ideas for enhancing the book.

I have added chapters on experimentation, historical research, comparative research, and participant observation to provide additional techniques for students to employ. The subjects and projects I offer for each of these methodologies are only suggestions; I know that many instructors ask their students to investigate different topics when they employ the various techniques described in this little book.

For those who might be interested, I've written other books that explore different research techniques—semiotics, psychoanalytic theory, Marxist theory, and sociological theory—for analyzing popular culture and the mass media. In these books (which include *Media*

*Analysis Techniques, Cultural Criticism: A Primer of Key Concepts,* and *Seeing Is Believing: An Introduction to Semiotics*), I explain these techniques and methodologies and apply them to everything from the television series *The Prisoner* and perfume advertisements to football and detective novels. I tend to use whichever technique, or combination of techniques, I think will be most useful in any given research effort (if you want to call what I do research, that is).

In one of my books, written a number of years ago, I was being frivolous and ironic when I wrote, "I don't do research; I just make everything up as I go along and throw in charts to make social scientists happy." Unfortunately, a number of people took me at my word, or pretended to, because I've gotten a lot of ribbing from my colleagues about not doing research. My point in mentioning this is to illustrate that *research* is a very broad and vague term. As I explain to colleagues in other departments, "When you watch television, you're wasting time; when I watch television, I'm doing research!" The fact of the matter is, a good deal of the time when I watch television, I actually *am* doing research.

I am grateful for Margaret Seawell's encouragement, and for all the comments and suggestions made by various scholars (some known to me, others anonymous) that have helped me write this second edition of *Media Research Techniques.* I hope it will do an even better job than the first edition of assisting students and others who wish to experience the fascination, and sometimes even the excitement, of research.

Let me close with a quote from Steven J. Rosenstone, dean of the College of Liberal Arts at the University of Minnesota, on the excitement involved in research. In the spring 1997 issue of the college's publication *CLA Today,* he writes:

> For me research involves the delicious (though sometimes painful) process of learning and discovery, and the indescribable exhilaration that comes from new insight and fresh ideas. . . . my research proceeds out of the conviction that there is always a more robust and compelling way to make sense of the human condition.

If you are interested in finding new ways of making sense of the human condition, I'd say you have the makings of a researcher, whatever your field.

# Part I
## Research Projects

My Illustrious Friend and Joy of my Liver!

The thing you ask of me is both difficult and useless. Although I have passed all my days in this place, I have neither counted the houses nor have I inquired into the number of inhabitants; and as to what one person loads on his mules and the other stows away in the bottom of his ship, that is no business of mine. But, above all, as to the previous history of this city, God only knows the amount of dirt and confusion that the infidels may have eaten before the coming of the sword of Islam. It were unprofitable for us to inquire into it. O my soul! Seek not the things which concern thee not. Thou camest unto us and we welcomed thee: go in peace.

reply of a Turkish official to an Englishman's
questions, quoted in Austen H. Layard, **Discoveries
in the Ruins of Nineveh and Babylon** (London, 1853)

# Chapter 1

## Guided Research Projects

Many people are confused about research. They have fantastic ideas and crazy notions about what research is and who conducts it. An episode of the *Nova* television series on quarks, for instance, showed physicists and other scientists looking for an "elusive" submicroscopic particle and using huge devices that cost hundreds of millions of dollars. When many of us think of research, images of such scientists, or of chemists in laboratories or of physicists with gigantic particle accelerators, probably pop into our minds. Or we may visualize psychologists working with subjects who are hooked up to some kind of complicated device. We see research in these terms because that is how scientists, who we know conduct "research," tend to be presented by the media. But what about English professors? Do they do research? Or philosophers? They read books and write articles, but is that research?

### What Is Research?

Let me suggest that research covers a much wider sphere of activity than you might at first imagine. The term research comes from the French word *rechercher*, which means to investigate something thoroughly, to search for information, to try to find out about something that is of interest. Research is also, to the extent possible, objective, carefully done, and conducted using methods that can be repeated. (These considerations will be discussed in greater detail in a short while.)

It is in these respects that research differs from what we do, without thinking much about it, in our daily lives. There is a famous passage in a play by Molière in which a rich aristocrat asks his philosophy master to write something expressing his love for a beautiful young lady. When the philosopher asks whether the note should be in poetry or prose, the aristocrat says it should be neither, that he wants something else. The philosophy master then explains that everything is either poetry or prose, and the aristocrat discovers, to his amazement, that he has been speaking prose all his life. All of us, let me suggest, are researchers—though we may not think of ourselves as such.

For example, suppose you wish to buy a new car and can afford one that costs $15,000. How do you find the best one for your needs? You might ask friends about their cars. You might go to the library and look at magazines about cars or *Consumer Reports.* You might look in newspapers for articles about automotive safety, new models (and their good and bad points), and so on. All of this is research.

This book will guide you through a number of specially designed research projects so that you can get a sense of the excitement that comes from actually doing research and discovering things. But before you start doing research, let me say something about the nature of research and the problems a person faces in conducting research.

## Aspects of Research

Some of the basic questions we ask when we do research are discussed below. Frequently we cannot provide answers to these questions that everyone will accept, but these are the kind of questions that researchers think about.

### The "Who" Question

Who was the first person to do something (run a mile in less than 4 minutes) or the last person to do something (climb Mount Everest)? Who is responsible for something happening, and how can we demonstrate or prove this? For example, who was "responsible" for the disaster in the savings and loan industry? Can we point a finger at any one individual or group of individuals or institutions?

## The "Why" Question

Why did something happen (the Civil War, World War I, the Great Crash of 1929, the Iran-contra hearings)? Why do some people with AIDS live for many years, whereas others die very quickly? Why are there so many homeless people? Why can't American automobile companies build cars that are as good as the ones built by Japanese companies? Why do people buy mink coats? Why are some people creative and others not?

When we answer a "why" question, we must offer evidence that an objective person might consider reasonable. Often we discover that there are a number of different answers, and it is difficult to determine which one is correct or explains things best.

## The "How" Question

How does some process work? How do we solve some problem? How did a certain situation develop? For example, we might wonder about how we can deal with the drug problem, or how we can prevent teenagers from dropping out of school, or how exclusive colleges determine which applicants to accept.

## The "What" Question

We ask a "what" question when we want to get information, quantitative data about particular phenomena. This is often a "what is the extent of" question, but it can also be a "what is the situation or what happened" question. For instance, television stations earn revenue by charging advertisers for running commercials during given programs, so advertising agencies, as might be expected, want to know what size audience can be expected to watch a particular program and what the audience might be like. For example, a 30-second commercial aired during the 1997 Super Bowl cost on average $1.2 million to reach an audience of some 140 million viewers. When you are paying that kind of money for a commercial, it is only logical to advertise products that members of that particular audience might be persuaded to use. That is why Super Bowl broadcasts include so many commercials for colas and none for Rolls Royces.

### The "When" Question

Here we are interested in time and the way time affects some process or sequence of activities or behaviors. We might wonder when some process starts or ends, or when is the best time to do something or prevent something from happening. When (at what age) do children tend to start smoking and taking drugs? When is the best time to educate children about drug abuse? What is the most effective age for sex education? When is the best time to teach children to read or to enroll children in school? When do people make up their minds about how they will vote?

### The "Which" Question

We ask a "which" question in trying to determine what factor or element in some group of factors or elements is significant or most important. This involves selecting from among alternatives. (In the case of buying a car, we might be torn between styling and safety features.) Which gene is most important in determining some disease? Which medicine is most effective in preventing some disease? Which procedure is best to follow after a mild heart attack? Which factors best predict success in college education?

### The "Where" Question

Just as "which" questions involve choices among alternatives, "where" questions involve location. Where does something happen? Where is some grouping that one might not expect to occur naturally? Where is the source of something, or where is the result of something felt? Where in the brain are the sources of some neurological problem? Where is oil buried? Where should the new state university be located so it will be most useful to the greatest number of people?

### A Complicating Factor

What makes research so difficult (and so fascinating) is that we often find that all of the questions discussed above are all mixed up together.

It is frequently impossible to isolate just one element in the puzzle; a researcher must be able to figure out how to estimate the weight to be given to "why" and "how" and "when" and "which" elements.

Social scientists must deal with people, who are very complicated, often don't know why they do things, and don't lend themselves to the kind of "hard" or "pure" research that is done in the physical and biological sciences. And physical and biological scientists find themselves dealing with phenomena of awesome complexity. Researchers in the arts and humanities have to deal with the still mysterious phenomenon of creativity and related factors.

In short, every researcher faces difficulties, whether in the physical or biological sciences, the social sciences, the arts and humanities, or the business world. Although we have discovered a great deal, there is an enormous amount we don't know—and, ironically, the more we discover, the more questions we raise for other researchers.

## The Game Element in Research

You may have noticed that in my discussion of research I use terms such as *discover* and *excitement*. That is because research is best understood as being like a game. There is a task, there are rules, and there is need for imagination and creativity. Research involves curiosity, accuracy, honesty, and ingenuity. Research is a process, an activity that includes thinking up interesting projects to work on and discovering ways of finding answers to questions—ways that involve ingenuity and imagination, as well as honesty in presenting one's findings.

The term *finding* is important. Researchers are looking for answers and never can be sure where they'll find them or what they'll find. The detective or spy metaphor is useful here. A researcher is a detective or a spy who is out to discover or uncover something that is, in some way, unnoticed, hidden, secret, or problematic. Researchers, like detectives, find that their sources sometimes lie, sometimes offer conflicting stories, and sometimes behave in baffling ways. That is why research is so exciting and why researchers often spend incredible amounts of time at their work.

This book offers a number of guided research projects that require you to make use of real (if somewhat simplified) research techniques, such as content analysis, surveys, and depth interviews. Each project has been designed to be conducted in a short period of time by all students (regardless of major) and at no expense. All of the projects present the same kinds of problems that professional researchers face when they conduct research.

Many students never have the opportunity to conduct research. The most they do are "term papers"—library research projects in which they investigate some subject by finding quotations from relevant experts and authorities and, in essence, stringing the quotations together in a report. These projects are based on the research of others, and so are one step removed from the actual research process as it is conducted in the humanities and social sciences. Doing a term paper is a useful exercise, and a standard mode of operation, but it does not give a student an understanding of what real research is like or an appreciation for the fascination research can generate. There is a library search (or documentary) exercise in this book, but what it requires from the student is slightly different from the conventional library research paper.

### Some Characteristics of Research

Research is generally understood to involve observation. The difference between the kind of observation and information gathering we do in everyday life and the kind we do in "formal" research is that in the latter we are more careful, more systematic, and more analytic, and we generally deal with more complicated matters. Let me discuss these characteristics of formal research in more detail.

1. In doing formal research, we observe things more systematically and try to be much more careful about our observations than in other situations. Observation is a key factor in much research, and correct observation involves, among other things, knowing what to look for, what to focus attention on, and what to ignore. Researchers may find ways to quantify their observations and may keep careful records of their observations.

Researchers also use concepts—ideas that help humans organize and make sense of things. Concepts do several things. They help us to see relationships between and among elements that may have previously escaped us, and they lead us to insights. For example, we need the concept of "violence" to find a way of dealing with such things as people threatening, striking, and/or shooting one another. Researchers have explored the relationship between violence on television and the behavior of people who watch television. Does televised violence "cause" violent behavior? This is a very complicated issue, with researchers arguing over how to define violence and how to determine whether the effect of watching televised violence is "significant." The matter has not been settled yet, and research on the subject goes on.

2. We are (or try to be) more objective in conducting research and in interpreting our findings than we are in ordinary life. Researchers who study how much television people watch (breaking audiences down into groups based on age, sex, education, and other factors) are concerned with getting accurate information. These researchers may not like television, may feel that it is junk, but their personal feelings and attitudes should not interfere with their desire to obtain accurate information about who watches television and how much television they watch.

3. In conducting research, we must be concerned with the typicality or atypicality of whatever it is we are studying. Is what we are investigating unique and unusual, or is it part of normal, everyday life? If we use a subject sample, we must try to obtain one that is representative, otherwise the information we get in our surveys or questionnaires (asking for political opinions, opinions about sexism and racism in the media, or whatever) will be distorted and misleading.

4. We must interpret our findings correctly and try to derive some kind of conclusion or generalization that is logical and reasonable. Suppose, for example, you do library research on the "punk" phenomenon. You read articles and books by psychologists (the punk psyche), sociologists (punks and social class), psychiatrists (punks and the absent father), and political scientists (punks and alienation). You should try to come to some conclusions about what punks are like, why people become punks, and what the existence of the punk subculture suggests about American culture and society. Because there is always room for error, you should state your conclusions in a tentative manner, qualifying them—but you should try to find some conclusion or

generalization of interest from your research. And you must be scrupulously honest about reporting your conclusions, whether they confirm or prove false any hypothesis you might have entertained.

## People Are the Craziest Monkeys

What makes media research so difficult (and so challenging) is that people are very complicated and hard to figure out. For example, suppose you construct a questionnaire and go around surveying people. Any of the following might take place:

- People will tell you what they think you want to hear.
- People will lie—they won't tell you what they actually think.
- People won't know what they think and will just give you some answers to get rid of you.
- People will tell you what they actually think, but they may not have any information, so what they think might not be very useful.
- People will tell you their opinions and these opinions will be based on information.

There are other problems as well. As a rule, human beings are not careful observers of events. Five people who see an accident might give five considerably different accounts of it. The brilliant Akira Kurosawa movie *Rashomon* is about the different descriptions people give of an incident. A notorious bandit overcomes a man, ties him up, and then has sex (in front of him) with the man's wife. Afterward, the husband dies. Everyone involved in the matter tells a different story: We don't know whether the woman is raped or seduces the bandit, or whether the husband is killed fighting the bandit, dies accidentally, or commits suicide. In the film we hear conflicting accounts by the wife, the bandit, the husband (via a ghost summoned to testify), and a woodcutter who observed what went on. We might call this matter of obtaining different accounts of an event the "*Rashomon* phenomenon." It poses an interesting question: Who do we believe when everyone tells a different story?

## Research in the Broadcast Industry:
## A Personal Perspective

The week I started writing the first edition of this book, I was interviewed by a reporter from a local television station. The reason I mention this is to emphasize an important point: Research is not something done only by scholars; it also plays an important part in the news and entertainment media. The reporter was working on a series of three 2-minute segments (to be shown on the late evening news) dealing with nostalgia in American culture. A producer for the reporter's news show had noticed that a number of TV commercials being run at the time had a "fifties" theme to them, and that there seemed to be a good deal of "back to the fifties" material reflected in our popular culture. Her question was, "Why is this going on, and why now?" (We will assume that she was correct about her nostalgia hypothesis.)

To find answers, the reporter called a number of universities looking for people who might have some "expertise" in this subject. She called the Public Affairs Office at San Francisco State University, which referred her to me, because I have done a considerable amount of work on media and popular culture. She also called Stanford University, where someone suggested she speak to a member of a local futures research organization, so she ended up interviewing a futurist. She called advertising agencies and all kinds of other people. She also found some articles and books that were relevant.

What this reporter did is, from my point of view, research. The success of reporters is as much connected to their ability to find information and good sources for interviews as it is to their ability to write and to speak well. This reporter's particular kind of research involved finding experts, people who could speak (allegedly, at least) with authority, and what she did was no different from what students do when they do library research projects, except that she did not rely on books and articles by experts or authorities, but went out and actually interviewed the experts.

So research is not some abstract process that is irrelevant to work and to life. It plays an important part in both, whether one does research on what automobile to buy, on the best way to get people to purchase some product or service, or on how to get a particular job.

## The Goal of This Book

This book deals with what might be called applied or "practical" research. It will lead you, step by step, through a number of research projects that will help you learn how to conduct research. The goal is not to turn you into a professional researcher, but to help you understand something about research so that you can function more effectively when you are working—regardless of the position you hold. We live in an information society; more than half of the U.S. gross national product comes from the processing of information. Given this situation, your ability to find information and interpret and evaluate it (whether you are a reporter, a producer, or an executive) is of great importance.

This book can be used in conjunction with texts on research methodology, but it can also stand alone; it can be used in courses on such topics as media, the popular arts, and American culture or society. It offers specially designed projects that can be done reasonably quickly and at little or no expense. The projects can be adapted or modified depending on the needs and interests of instructors and their students. For example, in the chapter on social role analysis (Chapter 5), instead of investigating soap operas, students can substitute some other genre. In the same manner, the concepts discussed in the chapter on rhetorical analysis (Chapter 7) can be applied to other media and other genres.

The detective metaphor is (once again) useful here. Research, in many respects, is similar to what detectives do. A detective has a crime to solve. He or she searches for clues, considers a number of suspects, and uses any clues uncovered to determine who is the guilty party (in mystery stories, usually a murderer). A researcher identifies some problem of interest, searches for information, considers how useful or correct the information is, and uses the information to come to some kind of conclusion or generalization. Researchers sometimes develop hypotheses (informed guesses) to test, but this is not always the case. Sometimes researchers investigate topics or problems that are of personal interest to them, that they believe have important and interesting implications. These parallel lists show some of the similarities between the detective and the researcher:

| *detective* | *researcher* |
|---|---|
| crime | problem, topic |
| clues | information |
| suspicious characters | questionable data |
| discovery of criminal | conclusion, generalization |

Why should students, to continue with the detective metaphor, only read about other detectives when they can be detectives themselves?

The work in the comparative study of lives brought another type of evidence in favor of using a personal journal as the basic instrument of personal growth. It was impressive to observe the number of persons in other cultures and other periods of history who have spontaneously kept a journal of some sort to meet various needs in their lives. These journals are primarily a chronological record of events. They are diaries elaborated to a greater or less degree depending on the temperament of the person and his life situation. Sometimes they are focused on a particular area of experience or a particular task, as is often the case for artists and novelists. In those cases a journal serves as the spontaneous psychological tool that makes it possible for the inner creative side of a work in progress to be carried through.

Ira Progoff, **At a Journal Workshop: The Basic Text and Guide for Using the Intensive Journal** (1975, p. 23)

# Chapter 2
## Research Logs

Keeping a research log is a subject dear to my heart, because I have been keeping something like a log—a journal—since 1954, and have written more than 50 journals since that time. Most of my books, including this one, have come out of my journals. The term *keeping* is very important, for it suggests some kind of obligation, a sense of duty. You have to be faithful to your log and spend time writing in it regularly or it will be of little value to you.

A distinction should be made here between a research log and a diary. A diary, as it is generally understood, is a record of personal thoughts, of private experiences, that focuses upon activities one is involved with, hopes, aspirations, matters of the heart, and that kind of thing. A log, on the other hand, is much different. A log may occasionally deal with personal matters, but its main focus should be on thoughts and reflections.

As you undertake the various research projects in this book, you should keep a log to record your thoughts and speculations about the projects. In this log you will "talk to yourself" about the problems you face in doing the research projects, ideas relative to the projects, what your findings mean, and other things of that nature.

Keeping a journal or log is a very effective way of forcing yourself to think about things and to maintain an "internal dialogue." The "writing across the curriculum movement" stresses the role that writing, and in particular journals and logs, can play in all courses—whether or not they are specifically designed as writing courses. For example, students in physics courses can record their thinking as they work on problems. When instructors examine their students' logs, they can see how the students dealt with the problems, see how their minds worked. When students have made errors, these will be reflected in their logs.

In the first chapter of *Improving Student Writing: A Guidebook for Faculty in All Disciplines,* Andrew Moss and Carol Holder (1988) discuss the value of writing:

> Whatever kinds of writing tasks you are at present assigning your students—research papers, essay exams, lab reports, book critiques, journals—your assignments are giving them a unique and valuable opportunity to learn. Through writing, students can learn to review and reflect upon the ideas they express, can learn to analyze concepts and see their relationships to one another. Unlike conversation, writing creates a visible record that one can ponder, add to, or revise. By challenging students to be analytical and reflective, well conceived writing assignments deepen their understanding of any field, enabling them to create meaning out of raw data and express that meaning intelligently to others. (p. 1)

What these authors say about writing in general is particularly relevant to the matter of keeping research logs.

## Difficulties in Log Writing

You must be disciplined about keeping a log—that is, you must write in it regularly. One thing you will discover, if you get into keeping a log, is that frequently the process of writing seems to take over, and all kinds of ideas, notions, and solutions to difficulties that were not in your consciousness when you started pop into your mind. As you become involved in the writing, many of your inhibitions ("That's a silly idea" or "That's too far out") slip away and you have access, somehow, to parts of your unconscious.

You have to be honest with yourself as you write in your log. You must be willing to record such things as difficulties, errors you may have made in some part of some research project, and problems you face. It is often difficult for people to be so honest. Also, you may find that your progress is uneven—sometimes things go well, other times everything goes wrong. Your log should reflect all this.

## Advantages of Logs

Logs are very "immediate," reflecting things as they evolve. Thus your log will provide you with a record of how you progressed as you worked on each of the various research projects assigned to you. As you keep your log, you can speculate on how things are going, record what you have found, and consider various aspects of your research. Being able to look back at this material will be very useful to you when the time comes to write up your findings.

Keeping a log is inexpensive and should not take a great deal of time. All you need is a bound laboratory notebook with numbered pages, a pen, and 10 or 15 minutes every day. What is important is that you write in your log regularly, not that you write in it for long periods of time. When you are done with your log, you will have an excellent record of your experiences in the course, and you may have ideas that you can develop into other research projects, future papers, and more.

## Guidelines for Keeping a Log

The following guidelines are based on my years of keeping journals and reflect my personal notions of the best ways to keep a journal or a log. There is no one way to keep a log, and your instructors may have their own ideas about journals and logs.

1. Keep your log in a bound notebook with numbered pages. You must not be able to tear pages out or add pages. Having the pages numbered means you can create an index in the back of the book, so you will be able to find what you have written in the log on given subjects with relative ease.
2. Write in ink—it is much easier to read than pencil. You can cross words out and be messy if you want; neatness is not a critical factor. Write directly into the log; don't write things out first on a separate piece of paper and then copy what you have written into your log. It is better to spend 20 minutes writing (and thinking) in a messy manner than 10 minutes writing something and another 10 minutes copying what you have written into your log. This is boring and wastes your time.
3. Note the date each time you write. This will enable you to see, at a later date, how you were progressing and when you were involved with various parts of each research project.

4. Make use of diagrams and charts. These show relationships and can be very useful in helping you gain insights and come to conclusions.

5. Use modified outlines when you are brainstorming. You can divide a page into three or four vertical columns, for example, and do a great deal of brainstorming up and down the columns. You can also number the ideas you generate—then, later, you can take some of these ideas and put them into a more logical or useful order. You might want to keep lists of things to do while conducting a content analysis or some other project. Or you may want to think of ideas you'll need to deal with for a write-up of some project.

6. Write headlines in your log all in capital letters when you are thinking about specific topics. This will enable you to keep a better index, and having a headline to focus your thinking can also help you to think more clearly.

7. Include small drawings, an inch or inch and a half square, from time to time. Such drawings give your log visual appeal, and when they are related to your topic, they may also help stimulate your imagination and thinking.

## A Case Study

You may find it interesting to see how notes in a writer's journal or log evolved into a book. A number of years ago, when I was deeply involved in semiotics (the science of signs), I started a journal that I called, appropriately, *The Sign* (I always give my journals titles, for some reason). In this journal I devoted page after page to speculating about different aspects of signs. I spent weeks thinking of all the things I might write about signs. In the journal I wrote many pages of lists, charts, speculations, topics—anything that came into my head that was related to semiotics.

Once I had done this preliminary "thinking," I decided to write a short book, of 70 or 80 pages, based on these ideas. I was offering a seminar in semiotics and the media, and I thought my students would find the book useful. Using the material in my journal—the notes, charts, diagrams, and speculations—as an outline, I wrote a book titled *The Sign*, which was duplicated by the campus bookstore, and used it in my seminar.

I later sent a copy of *The Sign* to an editor who was looking for manuscripts on the media, and he suggested I might want to expand it into a real book, which I was more than happy to do. So my journal led to *The Sign* and *The Sign* led to a book, *Signs in Contemporary Culture:*

*An Introduction to Semiotics,* which was published by Annenberg-Longman (Berger, 1984).

Figures 2.1, 2.2, and 2.3 present reproductions of, respectively, a
page from my journal, a page from the duplicated book *The Sign,* and
a page from *Signs in Contemporary Culture.* And *Signs in Contemporary
Culture,* let me add, is no different from any of my other books—they
all sprung from my journals. The moral of this disquisition, then, is
that you should keep a good log for the course for which this book was
assigned—and if you think the process is useful, start keeping your
own journal.

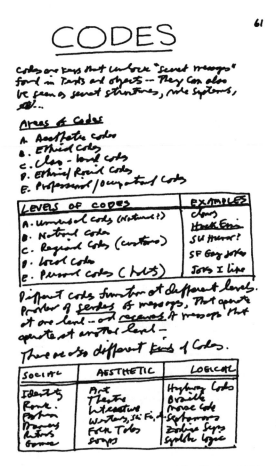

**Figure 2.1.** Page From Journal Used to Write *The Sign* and *Signs in
Contemporary Culture*

Berger
The Sign                        19

### 10. Levels of Codes

One of the problems we face in dealing with codes stems from the
fact that they can operate at different levels--sometimes at the same
time, also. Think of humor, for example. Some humor is universal--
things like the antics of clowns or mimes. Other humor seems to be
national or, at least, deeply affected by matters connected with
nations. Here I'm thinking of English understatement, American exuber-
ance, etc. Then, within nations, there are other subcategories such as
regional humor (Yankee, Southern), local humor (Bostonian) and
individual humor (a given person's sense of humor).

In the chart that follows I have categorized the levels of humor,
offered explanations of what causes them, and given examples.

| Level | Explanation | Example |
|-------|-------------|---------|
| Universal | Natural | Mimes, Clowns |
| National | History | American Characters |
| Regional | Geography | Country Bumpkin |
| Local | Groups | Jokes about Gays in S.F. |
| Individual | Personality | Jokes I like |

#### Code Levels

The fact that these code levels exist means that there is often a
great deal of confusion caused by, for instance, a sender of a message
operating at one level and a receiver of a message operating at another
level. In addition, matters such as educational level, ethnicity

**Figure 2.2.** Page From Typed Manuscript, *The Sign*

Then, within nations, there are other subcategories such as regional humor (Yankee, Southern), local humor (Bostonian) and individual humor (a given person's sense of humor). In the chart that follows I've categorized the levels of humor, offered explanations of what causes them, and given examples.

**Code Levels**

| Level | Explanation | Example |
|-------|-------------|---------|
| Universal | Nature | Mimes |
| National | History | American Characters, e.g. Huck Finn |
| Regional | Geography | Country Bumpkin vs. City Slicker |
| Local | Groups | Jokes about gays in San Francisco |
| Individual | Personality | Jokes I like |

The fact that different code levels exist means that there can be a great deal of confusion. For instance, the sender of a message can be operating at one level but the receiver of the message operating at another. In addition, factors such as educational level, ethnicity, social class, and race play a role and further complicate communication.

There is also the matter of kinds of codes. It has been suggested by the French semiologist Pierre Guiraud, in his book, *Semiology*, that there are three important kinds of codes: social codes, aesthetic codes, and logical codes.

The attributes and characteristics of these codes are found in the following chart.

**Kinds of Codes**

| Social Codes | Aesthetic Codes | Logical Codes |
|--------------|-----------------|---------------|
| Relations Among Men and Women in Society | Interpreting and Evaluating Arts and Literature | Understanding Nature and the World |
| Identity | Art | Highway Code |
| Rank | Literature | Symbolic Logic |
| Manners | Theatre | Braille |
| Fashion | Comic Strips | Morse Code |
| Rituals | Westerns | Sign Language |
| Greetings | Folk Tales | Sephamores |
| Games | Soap Operas | Zodiac Signs |

**Figure 2.3.** Page From *Signs in Contemporary Culture* (Berger, 1984)

Content analysis is a research technique for the systematic classification and description of communication content according to certain usually predetermined categories. It may involve quantitative or qualitative analysis, or both. Technical objectivity requires that the categories of classification and analysis be clearly and operationally defined so that other researchers can follow them reliably. For example, analysis of the social class memberships of television characters requires clear specification of the criteria by which class is identified and classified, so that independent coders are likely to agree on how to classify a character. . . . It is important to remember, however, that content analysis itself provides no direct data about the nature of the communicator, audience, or effects. Therefore, great caution must be exercised whenever this technique is used for any purpose other than the classification, description, and analysis of the manifest content of the communication.

Charles R. Wright, **Mass Communication:
A Sociological Perspective** (1986, pp. 125-126)

# Chapter 3

## Content Analysis:
## Newspaper Comics Pages

Content analysis, as the term will be used here, is a research technique that is based on measuring the amount of something (violence, negative portrayals of women, or whatever) in a representative sampling of some mass-mediated popular art form, such as a newspaper comic strip. (One can also conduct content analyses of phenomena that are not mass-mediated, such as personal letters, telephone conversations, and classroom lectures.) As George V. Zito writes in *Methodology and Meanings: Varieties of Sociological Inquiry* (1975):

> Content analysis may be defined as a methodology by which the researcher seeks to determine the manifest content of written, spoken, or published communications by *systematic, objective,* and *quantitative* analysis. . . . Since any written communication (and this includes novels, plays, and television scripts as well as personal letters, suicide notes, magazines, and newspaper accounts) is produced by a communicator, the *intention of the communicator* may be the object of our research. Or we may be interested in the audience, or *receiver* of the communication, and may attempt to determine something about it. (p. 27)

Content analysis is a means of trying to learn something about people by examining what they write, produce on television, or make movies about. Content analysts assume that behavioral patterns, values, and attitudes found in this material reflect and affect the behaviors, attitudes, and values of the people who create the material.

Zito also suggests that we can, perhaps, make inferences about the people who partake of the mass media—though there is a good deal of controversy about how much we can know about those who consume the mass media. Content analysis is an indirect way of making inferences about people. Instead of asking them questions, we examine what they read or watch and then work backward, assuming that what people read and watch are good reflections of their attitudes, values, and so on. We know that people interpret television programs in different ways, depending upon their backgrounds and education, so we cannot assume that everyone interprets (that is, responds to the content in) a given television show or movie the same way.

Generally speaking, when we do a content analysis, we try to obtain a substantial amount of material to examine, and we always do it from a comparative point of view. The crucial decision we must make is which categories to examine. For example, consider the matter of violence on television. If we are to examine violent content, we have to define what we mean by *violence*, decide whether "comic" violence is violence, when "insults" are violence, and whether accidents resulting in bodily harm are violence.

We would also want to know how much violence there is, relatively speaking, on television. For example, a content analysis of the amount of violence on television (or in the comics) at any given moment or period in time is not as useful as a content analysis that compares the amount of violence on television (or in the comics) at a given moment with the amount found 10 or 20 years ago. One reason we conduct content analysis is to determine whether or not there have been interesting changes over the years. We are looking for trends in such instances.

Content analysis might also be used to compare and contrast two different television programs (or two different kinds of programs) in the United States, or to compare television content across different countries. Sometimes we might focus our attention on such phenomena as basic values and attitudes, most important roles for men or women, or allusions to political or social matters found in a given television series or kind of program or comic strip or magazine. In all cases, however, we must quantify our findings—that is, deal with some element that can be counted.

## Problems in Conducting Content Analysis

There is a basic assumption implicit in content analyses, namely, that an investigation of messages and communication will make possible some insight into the people who create the messages and communication. These materials, we assume, provide vicarious experiences, inform, reinforce values and beliefs, and offer a variety of uses and gratifications.

On the most immediate level, the matter of defining terms is critical. For example, how do we define *violence*? Researchers of violent content in the media have to offer their definitions of the term, and there is a great deal of disagreement among researchers about what violence is and how it should be defined. Should intention to commit harm be classified as violence? If so, we can expect to find a good deal more violence on television than if we limit our understanding of violence to actual physical harm. And what about attempts to commit harm that are unsuccessful? What about verbal abuse? Is that violence?

What most researchers do is offer *operational definitions* of concepts or subjects they are investigating—definitions that contain descriptions of how the concepts are to be measured or counted. In the case of violence, for instance, we could say (for the purpose of a content analysis) that violence will be defined as any "actions and threats involving bodily harm done purposefully." It is often necessary to write rather involved operational definitions of terms or concepts being used in a content analysis. In the example just given, the notion of purpose is mentioned. That means that accidental harm or injury done to a person is not considered violence. And what about comic violence? Is slapstick to be considered violence? Clearly, if you define violence very narrowly, you will find little of it in any sample you examine; if you define it very broadly, you will find it everywhere. Where do you draw the line?

Another problem is that of finding a *measurable unit*, some standard way of analyzing your material. In doing a content analysis of a comic strip, it is reasonable to consider the frame as the standard unit. If you have a page with 10 strips on it and 4 frames in each strip, you have 40 frames to analyze. If you are doing a content analysis of newspaper articles, you can use something like column inches, as long as the columns are the same widths. If they are not, you have to make allowance for this by counting the actual areas in terms of square inches. But what do you do about television? Generally speaking, television researchers have used time units as their standard measure, and have investigated such things as the number of violent incidents per hour (after having defined violence operationally).

If you do not have a uniform standard measure that is easily quantified, your data (and remember, content analysis is a quantitative technique) will not be worth very much, because comparisons will be either impossible to make or meaningless. There is also the problem of *coder reliability*. Will everyone watching a given television program and counting the amounts and kinds of violence come up with the same figures?

### Advantages of Using Content Analysis

Content analysis is an inexpensive method of getting information about people. Using printed materials is inexpensive and relatively easy to do. Comics, for example, cost very little—and the same applies to magazines, newspapers, and other print media. Much of this material is available in libraries and on microfilm.

Content analysis also allows researchers to deal with subjects that are very current. They can work with the latest magazines or comic strips (and compare them with earlier ones), which means researchers can keep their fingers on the collective pulse, so to speak, and study phenomena as they develop—fads, fashions, crazes, and social movements.

If you have a decent library to use, you can also study the recent (and not-so-recent) past with considerable ease. This applies particularly to print media such as books, newspapers, and magazines. Many libraries have substantial collections of newspapers on microfilm, which means that obtaining material to subject to content analysis is not terribly difficult.

Content analysis is an unobtrusive method. One of the problems of doing research, we have discovered, is that the presence of researchers influences what they find. People act differently when they know (or even think) they are being observed. So content analysis is a way of avoiding the problem of researcher influence on individuals.

But we cannot completely escape the impact of the researcher on research design. As Gideon Sjoberg and Roger Nett point out in *A Methodology for Social Research* (1968):

> The researcher himself is a variable in the research design. He influences the course of any research he undertakes, and his actions are in turn structured by the broader society in which he lives. (pp. 2-3)

The implications of this statement are that even in content analysis, which is an unobtrusive method, the interests, beliefs, and maybe even the personalities of researchers are important, for these factors may play a role in determining what researchers choose to investigate. There is no escaping researcher influence, but in content analysis it is not direct, because mediated communication is being studied and not the behavior of people.

Finally, content analysis provides numbers. The technique is based on counting and/or measuring, and the findings are given in numerical form. Others can replicate the research and see whether or not they get the same numbers. If a content analysis is done correctly and the figures are accurate, replicated studies should obtain the same figures. But that is only part of the story, because once you have data, you have the problem of interpreting them.

## Disadvantages of Using Content Analysis

There is always a problem with sampling: How representative is the material one studies relative to all the material that could be studied? To get around this problem, content analysts often study a sizable amount of material. But what is the right amount of material to study, and how do you determine a reasonable way of sampling this material? For instance, how many hours of television should a researcher sample to determine, with any degree of accuracy, how much violence there is on television? Researchers usually get around this problem by selecting certain kinds of television programming that may be considered particularly important—children's television, prime-time network television, and so on.

How do we know that what researchers "find" in the material they analyze is what the creators of the material being analyzed "put into" it? At one time, communication researchers assumed that television viewers, for instance, were affected by (and tended to interpret) given programs in the same ways. This was known as the "magic bullet" theory. Shearon Lowery and Melvin DeFleur describe this theory in their book *Milestones in Mass Communication Research: Media Effects* (1983): "Early thinking about propaganda was that, like magic bullets, it struck all members of the mass audience equally and created uniform effects among them in a very direct way" (p. 105). Theorists now agree that individuals respond differently to the mass media and are not hit by magic bullets. People have different interests, educations, personalities, and backgrounds, and all of these factors play roles in how they respond to mass media.

In recent years, "reader response" theories have been developed, which suggest that "readers" (consumers of media) play a very important role in making sense of the media. Some theorists have even argued that readers play as important a role in finding meaning in media as "creators" do in making the material carried by the media. The point of all this is that we must be careful not to assume too much when we analyze our findings.

## Content Analysis Project: Newspaper Comics Pages

This research project is designed to make it possible for all students to undertake original research and obtain numerical and other data that they can then interpret. In certain cases, content analyses can be difficult to conduct, especially when one is dealing with attitudes and beliefs or other elements that are difficult to define with precision, or with topics that do not easily lend themselves to measurable units that are easy to work with. To avoid these problems, this project makes use of the comics pages in newspapers.

The purpose of this content analysis will be to see whether or not (and, if so, how) comics have changed over the years and what comics may reflect about changes in American culture and society. You will consider such things as the amount and kind of violence in the comics, the numbers of men and women in them, the numbers of words "spoken" by men and by women in them, allusions to social and political events, social and racial characteristics of the characters, and the attitudes and values displayed. (These categories form several

1. speech in regular balloons
2. thoughts in scalloped balloons
3. sound effects in zigzagged balloons
4. facial expressions
5. lines to indicate movement
6. panel for continuity
7. setting
8. art styles—light and dark, composition, and so on
9. language—meanings of words and punctuation
10. clothes, objects, and other examples of material culture

**Figure 3.1.** Decoding a Comic Strip Frame

concepts or constructs that you will use later to answer the research questions and interpret your findings.)

This exercise is similar in nature to the kind of research a communication scholar might undertake, except that it is much smaller in scale. It will also present you with a number of problems or dilemmas to deal with.

Figure 3.1 shows a sample comic strip frame and lists some things you will want to consider in decoding the elements in comics. Figure 3.2 is an example of a kind of chart you might want to use in conducting this content analysis; this format can be adapted to your particular purposes.

| 19___ | 19___ | Subject |
|---|---|---|
| | | number of strips on page |
| | | total number of frames on page |
| | | total number of characters (male and female) |
| | | number of male characters |
| | | percentage of male characters |
| | | number of female characters |
| | | percentage of female characters |
| | | total number of words spoken by all characters |
| | | number of words spoken by male characters |
| | | percentage of words spoken by male characters |
| | | number of words spoken by female characters |
| | | percentage of words spoken by female characters |
| | | total number of violent incidents per page |
| | | percentage of violent frames per page |
| | | references to politics, societal problems, and so on |
| | | other matters of interest: |
| | | |
| | | |

**Figure 3.2.** Content Analysis Chart for Newspaper Comics Pages

Carrying Out the
Content Analysis

1. Use a recent comics page from a local or regional newspaper (this should be a page from a Monday-through-Saturday edition). Cut it out of the newspaper and save it.

2. Obtain comics pages from the same newspaper from editions printed 20 to 40 years ago (or 30 to 60 years ago, or whatever your instructor suggests) to compare with the comics page you have on hand. You can photocopy microfilm pages or do the research at a microfilm machine. All your pages should be from approximately the

same time of year—that is, if you selected a page from your current newspaper during the first week in October, you should find copies of earlier comics pages from the first week in October.

If your instructor assigns different students different years to study, your class can cover a wide period of time. Newspaper comics have been around for more than 90 years, so as a class you can get a considerable amount of data on how they have evolved. Several students can be assigned the same time periods also; this is always interesting, because frequently different students end up with different statistics on everything from the number of frames on a page to the number of characters found in a strip.

3. Count the number of strips on each page, the number of frames on each page, the numbers of male and female characters on each page, the numbers of words the male and the female characters speak on each page, and the number of incidents of violence (and kinds of violence) on each page. When you count the numbers of male and female figures, you should count each time you see a male or female figure in a frame. That is, if you have a strip with four frames and the same male character appears in all four frames, for content analysis purposes that constitutes four male representations. Each time a male or female character appears, it is counted.

4. Determine the percentages of male and female figures, the percentages of words spoken by male and by female figures, and the percentage of frames with violence in them.

5. Figure out ways to describe and count the social characteristics of the characters other than sex—age, race, or whatever—to the extent this is possible, as well as allusions to social and political events, values, attitudes, and related concerns. Do you find patterns of dominance and submission? Are there interesting attitudes toward authority that you find? Are the differences in the kinds of violence you find ("serious" versus "comic") significant? How do you distinguish between them? Have there been significant changes in the kinds of strips found on the pages? If so, what are they? Why do you think they have occurred? How would you classify the strips on your two pages? Here, you must find classification systems that cover all the strips and whose categories are mutually exclusive.

6. List the problems you faced in making your content analysis and explain how you dealt with them. For example, how did you define *comic strip,* and how did you distinguish comic strips from cartoons that may also have been on the same pages? How did you deal with animals in the counts you made?

7. Write an essay about your findings and note the inferences or conclusions you came to based on your content analysis. This is an interpretive effort; it forces you to go beyond your data to try to figure out what your data on the changes in newspaper comics pages tell you about American culture and society. You should be able to use your statistics and other data to support your interpretations. Do not make things up—interpretation is not the same thing as invention.

Although this exercise simulates actual content analysis research, it does not require that you sample the comics systematically; for this reason, the generalizability of any results is questionable.

### Writing a Report on the Findings of Your Content Analysis

1. Write a brief introduction in which you give readers some background on the subject you investigated. Tell them what you wanted to find out, why you made your study, why it is important, and how you carried out your analysis. In writing this kind of a paper, the usual practice is to tell readers what you found at the beginning and then show them how you arrived at your conclusions. A research article is not structured like a mystery story, in which the secrets are not revealed until the very end.

2. Be careful to offer operational definitions of all important terms or concepts and to explain why the unit of measurement you used makes sense. That is, go into some detail on the technical aspects of the content analysis.

3. Present your findings in an easy-to-grasp manner—perhaps by using some kind of table that makes your findings clear. It may be useful to include with your write-up the comics pages you analyzed,

so readers can check on your findings. You will have to figure out how to classify the strips on each of your comics pages in some meaningful way.

4. Offer some hypotheses about what your results suggest. How do the two pages of newspaper comic strips reflect American culture and society? What effects do you think the comics have on readers? This kind of writing is speculative, but it is based on "hard" data—the statistics you have compiled.

Do not be put off by the fact that you must make inferences; this is always a problem when interpreting data. One way to deal with this problem is by qualifying your conclusions. You can write that your findings "would seem to indicate" or "suggest" a conclusion, rather than state that your findings "prove" some conclusion (which they likely do not). It is a good idea to avoid *all* and *every* statements, which suggest certainty. Also, avoid the word *proof*. It has been suggested that nothing in social scientific research is ever proven, nor do social scientists set out to prove anything.

5. Remember also to address any problems you had in making the analysis and explain how you dealt with them. For example, were certain racial and ethnic groups excluded or underrepresented in the comics you studied? How did you analyze allusions to social and political matters? What did you do about animals in strips? How did you decide on a classification system that was revealing (as opposed to one using such categories as "humorous" and "serious," which doesn't tell very much).

Content analysis is one of the more important techniques used in research concerning the mass media. The content analysis you have conducted is a smaller-scale version of the kind that research scholars do, and the problems and difficulties you faced are similar in nature to those that they face. There are many kinds of content analyses and many problems involved in conducting them. What you have done in your analysis of newspaper comics pages is "real" research, however. It is my hope that this exercise has intrigued you and whetted your appetite for doing other kinds of research, some of which are explained in the chapters that follow.

Opinion surveys are often dubious indicators of actual behavior because they do not, and perhaps cannot, measure the seething, changing, character of the public temper. They generally fail to embody the rich context of motivation and cross-communication out of which opinions arise and activate people in the mass. . . . The paradox of scientific method is that we change phenomena by measuring them. The confrontation of interviewer and respondent forces the crystallization and expression of opinions where there were no more than chaotic swirls of thought. The respondent's statements themselves represent a form of behavior; they are commitments. A question asked by an interviewer changes an abstract and perhaps irrelevant matter into a genuine subject of action; the respondent confronts a voting decision, exactly as he might on the choice of candidates or on a proposition in a plebiscite. The conventional poll forces expression into predetermined channels, by presenting clear-cut and mutually exclusive choices. To accommodate one's thoughts to these channels represents for the respondent an arousal of interest, an affirmative act.

Leo Bogart, **Polls and the Awareness of Public Opinion** (1985, pp. 17-18)

# Chapter 4

## Survey Interviews: Media Utilization

Surveys (in which researchers ask people questions and fill out forms of some kind) and questionnaires (forms that are presented or sent to people for them to fill out) are two of the most common ways of finding out what people think and do: their beliefs, their opinions, actions they've taken, actions they are contemplating, and so on. This is an example of descriptive research, research designed to find out such things as what products people use, how they intend to vote in forthcoming elections, and their positions on particular social or political issues. There are other kinds of interviewing that can be done as well, such as depth interviewing, which will be discussed in Chapter 6.

Surveys must be distinguished from experiments, which are another way of finding information. As Julian L. Simon writes in *Basic Research Methods in Social Science: The Art of Empirical Investigation* (1969):

> A survey gathers data about variables *as they are found in the world.* The survey can *observe behavior,* as for example whether or not people are athletes, whether or not they smoke, whether or not the money supply is high some years, and whether or not there is prosperity in those years. The survey can also collect data on what people *say*; for example, researchers can ask people of various backgrounds for whom they will vote or how much liquor they drink. The important distinction between the survey and the experiment is that the survey takes the world as it comes, without trying to alter it, whereas the experiment systematically alters some aspects of the world in order to see what changes follow. (p. 229)

In the exercise described below, you will construct an *instrument* (a social science term for a list of questions) and use it to find out how much time people spend with the mass media—watching television, listening to the radio and to recorded music—and why they spend time with the media.

One thing you must do when conducting survey research is find the "right" people to interview. If you want to know how students are going to vote in an upcoming election, you must find students who are eligible to vote. If you want to know how suburban housewives feel about some television program, you must get a representative sampling of suburban housewives. Finding the proper sample is not always easy to do.

You must be concerned, then, with two factors. First, you must consider the social and economic characteristics of your respondents (the people you will be interviewing): age, sex, race, religion, education, and occupation, among other things. Second, you must ask questions that will elicit useful information on the subject of your inquiry. Then, if you are lucky, you may be able to find correlations—that is, relationships—between, for example, occupation and voting intentions, or education and magazines subscribed to.

As Rubin, Rubin, and Piele write in *Communication Research: Strategies and Sources* (1990): "Survey research often employs a correlational design, not looking for cause-and-effect connections but seeking to describe the opinions or attitudes of certain groups, or the relationships between two or more factors" (p. 178). Correlations may not tell us why something occurs (that is, what causes it)—although they can, in certain circumstances—but they still can provide interesting material about relationships. When relationships are established, we may find, for example, that young people don't like talk shows, that senior citizens do like talk shows, and so on. Such information is useful to people who wish to advertise products that appeal to young people or senior citizens.

One must be careful, however, because correlations don't always work out as might be expected. For example, a television station in San Francisco had research data that viewers of *The Cosby Show* tended to watch a good deal of television news. So the station bought the rights to rerun *Cosby* (at great expense), and then found that its audience didn't like watching the reruns in the late afternoon, when they were originally scheduled (just before the evening news), nor did they watch the show when it was rescheduled after the 11:00 p.m. news. As a result of this experience, the station lost a number of its regular news viewers and a great deal of money.

## Problems With Surveys

When conducting survey research, you must define the topic you wish to investigate very carefully and precisely, because your topic will determine the questions you ask. That is, you must have a focus. Suppose, for example, that you want to obtain information for a politician running for office. You may want to find out how different groups perceive the candidate. Is there a difference between men and women in terms of how they feel about the candidate and her various policies? How do middle-aged and older people view the candidate? White people and people of color? Once you obtain this information, you can advise the candidate about the need to modify her policies or explain them more clearly.

You must figure out how to obtain a representative sampling of the social groups you want to survey. This is an important problem, because if you don't survey a representative sampling of your *population* (the technical term for a complete group of interest) your answers won't be worth very much. In the case of surveys made by professional polling organizations, relatively accurate information about the American public, some 260 million people, can be obtained by interviewing as few as 1,500 people. How can anyone possibly know what 260 million people think based on information from only 1,500 people? The answer is that these organizations use carefully selected representative samples that accurately reflect characteristics of the general population. This "magic" is based on probability theory. The basic idea is that error is always present when samples are used. The magnitude, or size, of the error is reduced, however, as the sample size increases— but only up to a point.

### An Example

Let me offer an example that is oversimplified, but will show how this works. Consider the figure on the next page, which is composed of 15 squares. If you know what a couple of the squares are like, you know what all the other squares are like.

In survey research, the "figure" is more complicated, but if you can find a representative sample of a certain size (based on obtaining random samples of a size that statisticians say is necessary), you can often obtain relatively accurate information—to within 3% one way or the other, and sometimes even less. According to statisticians, a sample that is twice or even 10 times as large as the typical 1,500 people would not be much more accurate.

We will assume (to simplify matters) that the sampling of people you use in doing your survey will be random and representative. You can try to find as many different kinds of people to interview as you can, to help things along, but a random sample is not necessary for this exercise.

## Advantages of Surveys

Conducting a survey is a relatively inexpensive way of obtaining information. You can ask a considerable number of questions, though you must be careful that you don't ask so many that your respondents become irritated.

If the sampling is correct, surveys and other forms of opinion polls are generally reasonably accurate. Pollsters have become very sophisticated in obtaining representative samples of people and all kinds of information.

Information can be obtained on past behavior and on future behavior (voting intentions, potential purchases, opinions on issues) that is useful to the parties conducting or paying for the surveys. As mentioned earlier, however, as in the case of the San Francisco television station that purchased *Cosby* reruns, sometimes this information can lead one astray. Sometimes unwarranted inferences are drawn from the information obtained in survey research.

Answers to survey questions can be represented in numerical form and subjected to various kinds of analyses. When information is obtained about the social characteristics of the respondents, the data can be used to make many correlations and to predict behavior in the general public. We see this during elections. Television networks and local stations employ pollsters who have developed sophisticated ways of sampling people as they leave voting booths. As a result of information obtained from these people (and based on the representativeness of certain districts), very often election outcomes can be determined even before the polls have closed. This has now become a point of contention between the media and many politicians, because a number of people feel that the early prediction of results may affect elections by dissuading people who have not voted from voting.


## Disadvantages of Surveys

In conducting survey research, getting a representative sampling is often difficult and can be very expensive. This is not a concern in the case of this exercise, however.

Also, because surveys must have some focus, they must be limited in scope. The list of questions must be fixed, and there is no room for maneuver, as in the depth interview.

The people who respond to surveys may not give honest answers; for example, they may fear that they won't look good if they tell the truth, or that the interviewer will have a negative opinion of them. This is particularly true where controversial issues are concerned; in such situations, the use of questionnaires is often a better choice. In answering survey questions, people often exaggerate their incomes, have mistaken notions regarding the social classes they belong to, lie about their ages, and claim to have voted for winners in elections (because they want to be on the "winning" side). They may also not really understand particular questions, but think they do. All these factors affect a study's validity and accuracy.

In real life, you should always find out whether anyone has recently conducted a survey on the same topic you propose to investigate. If so, there is no need to duplicate the survey. Also, it is a good idea to pretest your survey, to find out whether there are any problems with any of the questions: Are any of them confusing or ambiguous? Are any too personal for people to answer comfortably?

### Survey Interview Assignment: Media Usage Among Students

In this exercise, you want to find out how many hours, in a typical day, the students you survey spend watching television or VCRs, listening to the radio or CDs and tapes, and reading newspapers, magazines, or books. You should find it interesting to see, for example, how grade point average, age, sex, socioeconomic class, and other social characteristics correlate with media usage patterns.

We actually have a good deal of information, taken from national surveys, on this subject. You will want to compare your findings with the figures for the United States as a whole.

### Constructing a Survey

Constructing a survey is difficult, because all your questions must be unambiguous and perfectly clear to everyone, otherwise respondents will not be able to answer them correctly. Here are some considerations to keep in mind as you develop your survey on media usage:

1. *The order of the questions:* Do you ask "interesting" questions first, so your respondent will answer them, or do you start off asking questions about your respondent's social characteristics?
2. *The logic of the question order:* Some questions logically come before others. For example, you can't ask a person for an opinion about something until you first find out whether or not he or she knows anything about it.
3. *The utility of the questions:* You have only a limited number of questions you can ask (to avoid irritating your respondent), so you must ask questions that will elicit the information you need.
4. *How many questions to ask:* Is one question enough or are several needed? For clarity, you must limit each question to a single topic. This means that, in some cases, you must ask a number of related questions to obtain all the information you want.

5. *The respondent's ability to answer:* Will the respondent have the necessary information to answer your questions?

6. *The content of the questions:* Are any of the questions biased in some way? That is, have you, without being aware of it, "loaded" some of the questions so that certain answers will be given? Remember, *how* you ask a question plays an important role in the answers you get. To the extent possible, your questions should be neutral. Your task is to get other people's opinions, not to get them to agree with yours.

7. *The language used in the questions:* Are the questions worded clearly? Are all terms explained so that the respondent understands everything? Some respondents may be shy or may feel that asking about the meanings of certain terms will suggest that they are ignorant, and thus will give you answers to questions that they don't understand.

8. *The forms of the questions:* Which kinds of questions do you wish to ask? If you ask *open* questions, so respondents can give lengthy answers, it will be difficult to quantify what you find. If you ask *closed* questions, in which respondents select answers from choices you offer them, you may be oversimplifying things and not getting people's real opinions.

9. *The purposes of the questions:* Do you wish to measure intensity—how strongly people feel about issues—as well as opinions and beliefs and attitudes? If so, how do you do this?

10. *The clarity of the questions:* Have you created any "double-barreled" questions by mistake? These are questions that require single answers although they address more than one topic—for example, "How satisfied are you with television coverage of Europe and the Middle East?" The respondent may have different opinions about the coverage of Europe and the coverage of the Middle East, but has no opportunity to make that clear in his or her reply.

### Constructing a Survey Interview Instrument

For this exercise, construct an instrument that is designed to obtain information about how much time your respondents spend listening to or watching (or involved with) various media, and how they feel about and use the different media. Some things you might want to investigate include the following:

1. What do your respondents own in the way of color or black-and-white television sets, VCRs, stereos, compact disc players, boom boxes, radios, and so on? What do their families have at home?

2. How much time do they spend listening to or watching each of the various media? When do they partake of the different media?

3. Do they do other things while involved with the media? Do they listen to the radio or watch television while they do homework or chores around the house?

4. How do they use the media? To kill time? To entertain themselves? To relax? To find out what's going on in the world? To socialize with their friends? To deal with loneliness or stress?

5. What are their favorite radio stations and programs, television shows, magazines, and the like?

Be on the lookout for poor questions. If the answers you get are confused, or if you get many respondents saying they "don't know" or "don't understand," or refusing to answer particular questions, something is wrong. You should try to obtain information that is specific. For example, you should find out how many minutes or hours your respondents spend daily with each of the media and when in the day they tend to spend that time.

### Interpreting Your Findings

It would be best if you could interview 10 people about their media usage, trying to get as representative a sample as possible. If you want to find out about media usage among college students, for example, it would be good to interview two students from each of the various classes: freshmen, sophomores, juniors, seniors, and graduate students. Or you could narrow your focus and interview only members of your research class or some other class.

When you have finished your interviewing, consider how you might best present your findings. Can you create a chart that will show what you have found? Whatever format you choose, you should assemble your data in some logical way and then try to figure out what they mean. What do they suggest about the group you studied?

### Writing a Report on Your
### Findings From the Survey

1. Write a brief introduction telling what information you wanted to find, why you wanted to obtain this information, and what you found. Remember, you should state your conclusions at the beginning of your paper, not at the end.

2. Attach a copy of your survey so that readers can evaluate it in terms of its fairness and comprehensiveness.

3. Present your data in some easy-to-read format, giving the questions and the results of your survey. Make sure you connect your findings with the social characteristics of the people you studied.

4. Discuss the results of your survey and the conclusions you draw from them. Remember to qualify your answers and avoid sweeping generalizations.

5. Discuss any difficulties you faced in developing and conducting the survey, and explain what you did to overcome or compensate for them.

In . . . most . . . usages, the following elements appear in the definition of role: it provides a strategy for coping with a recurrent type of situation; it is socially identified, more or less clearly, as an entity; it is subject to being played recognizably by different individuals; and it supplies a major basis for identifying and placing persons in society.

Ralph Turner, "Role: Sociological Aspects," in **International Encyclopedia of the Social Sciences,** Volume 13 (1968, p. 552)

# Chapter 5

## Social Roles: Television Soap Opera Characters

The concept of "social role" comes from social psychology and means, in everyday language, the behavior that is expected of people, given their places in particular groups or organizations. A role is generally understood to be a persistent pattern of conduct that is always connected with a particular situation. The term *role* comes from the theater, where it means a part in a play.

When we look at the way people behave in terms of their roles, we may be described as adopting a theatrical or dramatic point of view; we see life as being like a play in which everyone is playing roles (and not necessarily being or revealing themselves). Sociologists who adopt this perspective sometimes call it a "dramatistic metaphor." This metaphor suggests that much of our behavior can be seen as a kind of acting for the benefit of others with whom we are involved, our "audience." We can look at people's behavior, then, in terms of the various roles they assume in the conduct of their daily lives. They are not necessarily conscious that they are adopting these roles, because their behavior patterns have become internalized and seem completely natural.

### The Focuses of Role Analysis

There are, then, two areas in which we can focus our attention in conducting role analysis: One is society, groups, and organizations, and the other is behavior. Society, in general, and groups and organizations, in particular, have a great deal of influence on the ways people act. One of the basic functions of our educational system and family life is to teach children how to play roles properly. Society functions

45

much more smoothly when people know what roles they are to play and how to play them than when there is confusion about roles.

We realize, also, that a given person may play many different roles during a typical day. Jane Q. Public might typically play the roles of parent (to her children), wife (to her husband), professor (to her students), administrator (to her colleagues), writer (to an editor), and so on. Roles are typically differentiated from status, which involves the amount of prestige and power an individual has in society or in some organization. Of course, the status a person has affects the roles that he or she plays.

### Final Definition of Social Role

If we put together all of the elements mentioned above, we arrive at our final definition of social role: A social role consists of a persistent pattern of conduct and behavior that is connected to the individual's position in some social structure or organization. A social role can be thought of as a link between a person's personality structure and the social structure (see Exhibit 5.1). Our parents generally spend a good deal of time teaching us how to play various roles.

Another way we learn roles is by observing "models," people we respect and admire, and imitating them in various ways. The importance of heroes and heroines (especially in the mass media) cannot be underestimated here. Most Americans watch about 3 hours of television a day and also spend a considerable amount of time listening to recorded music and watching films or videos, which means that we are exposed to large numbers of heroes, heroines, and other kinds of characters with whom we identify to varying degrees and in varying ways. One of the most important things roles do for us is help us to attain *identities*.

### Significant Others and Identity

When we play roles, we need others to respond to them in the correct manner—that is, in the way we intend them to be perceived. George Herbert Mead, a famous social psychologist, used the term "significant

---

**Exhibit 5.1**

Collective representations are the result of an immense cooperation, which stretches not only into space but into time as well; to make them, a multitude of minds have associated, united and combined their ideas and sentiments; for them, long generations have accumulated their experience and their knowledge. A special intellectual activity is therefore concentrated in them which is infinitely richer and complexer than that of the individual. From that one can understand how the reason has been able to go beyond the limits of empirical knowledge. It does not owe this to any vague, mysterious virtue but simply to the fact that according to the well-known formula, man is double. There are two beings in him: an individual being which has its foundation in the organism and the circle of whose activities is therefore strictly limited, and a social being which represents the highest reality in the intellectual and moral order that we can know by observation—I mean society. This duality of our nature has as its consequence in the practical order, the irreducibility of a moral ideal to a utilitarian motive, and in the order of thought, the irreducibility of reason to individual experience. In so far as he belongs to society, the individual transcends himself, both when he thinks and when he acts.

SOURCE: Durkheim (1965, p. 29).

---

others" to describe the people who respond to us and help us confirm our identities. In *Sociology: A Biographical Approach*, Peter L. Berger and Brigitte Berger (1972) write:

> The socialized part of the self is commonly called *identity*. Every society may be viewed as holding a repertoire of identities—little boy, little girl, father, mother, policeman, professor, thief, archbishop, general and so forth. By a kind of invisible lottery, these identities are assigned to different individuals. Some of them are assigned from birth, such as little boy or little girl. Others are assigned later in life, such as clever little boy or pretty little girl (or, conversely, stupid little boy or ugly little girl). Other identities are put up, as it were, for subscription, and individuals may obtain them by deliberate effort, such as policeman or archbishop. But whether an identity is assigned or achieved, in each case it is appropriated by the individual through a process of interaction with others. It is others who identify him in a specific way. Only if an identity is confirmed by others is it possible for that identity to be real to the individual holding it. (p. 62)

Roles, then, when they are confirmed by significant others, help to establish identity.

## Social Role and Counterrole
## Analysis of Soap Operas

The purpose of your research exercise concerning social roles is to determine what kinds of roles are assigned to men and women in a sampling of some representative television soap operas. What roles are emphasized and what roles are de-emphasized for men, women, African Americans, aged people, ethnic minorities, children, adolescents, and others? To carry out this assignment, you should consider such elements as the following:

1. the occupation of a character or the position a character has in some organization or group
2. the status a character has, which is tied to his or her position
3. counterroles of various characters (such as doctor-patient, clerk-customer) that complement particular roles
4. privileges and obligations connected to given roles (e.g., privileges and obligations of the head of a corporation versus those of a clerk-typist who works in the office pool of that organization)
5. perceptions of roles—how people's roles are envisioned in given situations and what these roles are as seen by others
6. performance of roles—how various characters perform their roles and how these performances are seen by others
7. conflicting roles—what happens when a character is torn between two different roles, when performing one role will interfere with performing the other
8. relations between roles and people's values, beliefs, and attitudes
9. role props—devices (clothes, hairstyles, language, eyeglasses, settings, and so on) used to define characters' roles

You should be aware of all these aspects of roles when you make your social role analysis of the television programs.

Roles played by people require others, acting in counterroles, to succeed. These roles and counterroles form what might be called scenes (and what you observe on television, when you watch your soap operas, will actually or technically be scenes). Figure 5.1 shows the roles and counterroles of a professor. As you can imagine, a professor plays different kinds of professional roles, depending upon whether he or she is speaking with the president of the university, a

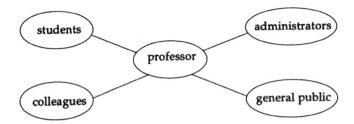

**Figure 5.1.** Roles and Counterroles of a Professor

student, a colleague (who may have higher rank), or staff people—secretaries, librarians, or technicians.

In carrying out your research, be sure to use a soap opera that has interesting characters who function as socially significant role models. After you describe the roles and counterroles of the characters you have studied, you should relate what you have found to society in general and to the social concerns most people have. You should speculate, for example, how these role models may be influencing people or may have influenced people. You might also want to say something about whether the heroes and heroines you have studied reflect basic American values and norms or something else.

## Problems in Social Role Analysis

A focus on social roles suggests that society is rather static. In static societies, people are awarded their status and roles by ascription (based on their families and connections) rather than based on achievement (on the basis of hard work). In most modern societies, however, things are rather fluid, and people change roles and identities from time to time—sometimes constantly.

Focusing on social roles may lead us to neglect other aspects of life—people's personalities, values, intelligence, character, and moral sensibilities. Thus we must be careful not to assume that people's social roles are the only important things to know about them. And because people vary their roles during any given day—professor, wife, mother, consultant—depending upon the situations in which they find themselves, we must be careful not to distort our understanding of them by neglecting certain roles and focusing on atypical ones.


## Advantages of Social Role Analysis

Observing social roles in television soap operas is inexpensive, and the material is easy to find and record. In addition, the genre is an important one. There has been a good deal of research conducted on television soap operas, and you should be able to find a number of books and articles in scholarly journals to use as background for your work.

Social role analysis offers insights into how society maintains itself. All societies provide people with a repertoire of social roles, which people frequently internalize and don't even recognize. These roles are connected with basic attitudes and values, so a study of social roles can be a useful means of formulating insights about American society. Consider dealing with some or all of the following topics:

1. demographics of characters: age, sex, occupation, education, race, ethnicity, socioeconomic class (to the extent you can determine these)
2. attitudes toward authority, members of the opposite sex, the family, work, power, racial minorities, ethnic minorities, and so on
3. basic goals, values, and beliefs of characters
4. moral sensibilities of characters
5. lifestyles of characters and what these imply

Because social roles as reflected in the mass media often function as models for people, who learn from these models how individuals behave in various roles (so social learning theory suggests), studying social roles can help us to find out how people see themselves—or, to be more accurate, how they are being taught to see themselves. For example, consider the roles given to women in soap operas. A great deal of the time, women in these programs serve primarily as sex objects; they are seldom shown in high-status occupations, are often portrayed as silly (or vicious), and generally do not provide satisfactory role models to the millions of women who watch (or for men either, who get ideas from such portrayals about how women should be treated). One of the basic goals of the women's liberation movement has been to change the ways women are portrayed in soap operas and other television programs, because these old roles provide unsuitable models for people of both sexes and all age groups.

## Disadvantages of Social Role Analysis

It is often difficult to determine accurately certain demographic aspects of the various characters in soap operas. We may know something about their occupations and can infer other things about them based on that knowledge, but we can't be certain. This is true in real life as well.

Also, soap operas have been on television so long that it is difficult to know what sample to use that would be truly representative. And the actions of soap opera characters are often so exaggerated and the characters so unusual that analyzing their role relationships may not provide insights about the roles and counterroles of ordinary people.

## Social Role Analysis Assignment

Analyze the roles and counterroles of the main characters in a reasonable sample of daily or evening soap operas; construct diagrams (as many as needed) to show the important roles and counterroles. Pay particular attention to the roles given female characters, how the characters establish their identities in the story, and how they use other characters to affirm these identities. Use the list of topics for consideration presented in the section on the advantages of social role analysis.

## Writing a Report on Your Role Analysis Research

1. Begin your report on your research with an introduction that gives your readers some background on the subject. Establish the context for your study by discussing the research on soap operas that has been conducted by others. Then present the conclusions you came to after you made your study.

2. Discuss the roles you observed and how you conducted your research. How many programs did you study? How many hours of television did you watch? Which roles, or aspects of roles, did you focus on? Why? What problems did you face in making your analysis? How did you solve them? You might also say something about the various props (clothes, houses, cars, hairstyles, objects of one sort or another) associated with particular characters to give others (including viewers) a sense of their roles and identities.

3. Make a diagram of the important roles and counterroles you studied. You might offer brief descriptions of the plots of the episodes you studied, to give readers a sense of what you saw and to make your diagram more easily understood.

4. Tie your research to findings by others about soap operas in general and your soap opera in particular. (Many articles about soap operas have appeared in the *Journal of Communication* and other scholarly journals, and a number of books have been published that discuss particular soap operas and soap operas in general.) You should say something about how your findings relate to the work done by other scholars in this area. One interesting question to consider is whether or not the roles of women have changed in significant ways over the past decade or so in soap operas and in the mass media in general. Depending upon how much time you have, you might also investigate work by sociologists and other social scientists on role model theory in general.

Be alert to the kind of information your informant is conveying to you. Is it his or her analysis of the topic or a pure description of it? Is this the informant's perspective or that of someone else? Is your informant being honest, or manipulating the material to impress you (are there ulterior motives involved)? Anytime there is a sense of discomfort in the atmosphere, try to pinpoint its cause. . . . When you have located an appropriate informant, one who is cooperative, knowledgeable, and reliable, there are various considerations for the interview itself. The place where the interview is to occur must be selected carefully. It should be convenient both to researcher and informant. It should not be too noisy, because the ethnographer must pay close attention to the interview, and of the requirements of tape recording, if such is to be used.

Lebriz Tosuner-Fikes, "A Guide to Anthropological Fieldwork on Contemporary American Culture," in Conrad Phillip Kottak (Ed.), **Researching American Culture** (1982, pp. 27-28)

# Chapter 6

## Depth Interviews: Favorite Singers and Recordings

In the research assignment for this chapter, you will investigate people's favorite singers and recordings and try to find out why those people like certain singers and songs. You will do this by conducting depth interviews. A depth interview is really an extended conversation, but it has a different purpose from that of an ordinary conversation. In a typical conversation, people talk about their work, their families, events in the news, people they know, and so on. The conversation can ramble and move in many different directions. The depth interview, in contrast, is highly focused. It is conducted to get at particular issues, such as hidden feelings or attitudes and beliefs of which a respondent may not be aware or that are only dimly in his or her consciousness.

A depth interview is a kind of probe. When conducted by trained interviewers, many of whom have advanced degrees in psychology, depth interviews can sometimes last an hour or more. The reason such interviews can take so much time is that it is often necessary to penetrate the defenses people put up to prevent their hidden beliefs from coming to light—defenses that they frequently are not conscious of and do not recognize in their behavior.

Depth interviewing is often done for commercial reasons—to find out why people purchase one brand of coffee and not another, how they feel about cake mixes, or why they use cigarette lighters. Ernest Dichter, the father of motivation research, has written a number of books that are full of what was discovered when depth interviews were conducted about various products—everything from fur coats to brands of soup.

### Focus Groups and Oral Histories

Sometimes focus groups are used to find out the opinions of a number of people about some product. This form of group interview is not the same as a depth interview; the information obtained in focus groups reflects group opinions and attitudes rather than hidden beliefs. A focus group research assignment is presented in Chapter 9, where this form of interview will be discussed in more detail.

The oral history, collected with a tape recorder, may be seen as a modified form of the depth interview. The reasons for conducting depth interviews are vaguely similar to those for collecting oral histories, but in oral histories the focus is on the individuals' experiences and what these experiences reveal about particular periods in history or the lives of the individual subjects. In collecting oral histories, researchers try to get subjects to provide detailed recollections and anecdotes (and, in some cases, songs, poems, folklore, and the like) that can give personal perspectives on history and the way people lived in earlier times or in particular places and circumstances.

### Problems With Depth Interviews

You may have difficulty getting the right respondents for your project. Some of the people you interview may be shy or may be otherwise reluctant (for various reasons) to talk freely with you, so you may not get the kind of information you are looking for. Some interviewees will talk around any subject and are hard to pin down; others are afraid to express their feelings.

Also, it is sometimes difficult to maintain a depth interview long enough to elicit any real answers. For this assignment, a 15- or 20-minute interview will do, but even that may be difficult to maintain. Of course, if you have the time and a good respondent, you can do a much longer interview, perhaps as long as an hour.

You may not know precisely what it is you are looking for in your depth interviews, other than that you are trying to find out whether your respondents have any hidden reasons that explain why they like the singers they do and buy the CDs and tapes they do. You probably also won't know what you've found until you have analyzed your notes from a number of depth interviews and discovered what, if anything, they reveal.

## Advantages of Depth Interviews

You can collect a great deal of detailed information when you conduct depth interviews. You can ask follow-up questions and pursue topics that interest you for a considerable length of time.

In conducting such interviews, you often obtain unexpected information that other forms of research might not discover. Sigmund Freud argued that slips of the tongue and the dreams people have can be useful sources of information about their mental states that other kinds of research cannot get at. He developed a method called *free association*, in which he asked his patients to tell about their dreams and whatever else came into their heads. Depth interviewing can be seen as an adaptation of this technique. The more people talk, the more they reveal (give away) about themselves. In the depth interviewing you will do for this assignment, you will not be concerned with analyzing people, but with finding out why people like the singers they do and buy the recordings they do.

When conducting a depth interview, you can adapt as the situation changes. If a promising topic comes up, you can pursue it. You can ask the respondent to be more specific or to try to generalize, whichever will be most useful to you.

The topics you will investigate in this assignment are of widespread interest. Many people have stereo systems and extensive collections of music tapes and compact discs, and many people listen to the radio for hours at a time and follow the newest releases. The subject, then, is important to many young men and women and is one about which many will be happy to talk.

## Disadvantages of Depth Interviews

It can be difficult to handle the enormous amounts of material that depth interviews can generate. It is possible to obtain a great deal of information during each interview, and if you conduct a number of such interviews, you can face formidable amounts of data.

If you use a tape recorder in your interviews, normally you would transcribe this material, a procedure that is very time-consuming. In this particular case, because this is a student research exercise, you will not be asked to transcribe your tapes.

Finally, it is not always possible for respondents to give meaningful answers in depth interviews. Moving from discussing *what* they have done to *why* they did it is not easy for many people, especially because some people don't always know why they take certain actions. In this case, they may know what singers and recordings they like, but they might not know why they like them.

### Depth Interview Research Project

The subject of your depth interviews is the preferences people have for particular singers and recordings. Music is something that plays an important part in our lives and about which many people have strong and definite feelings and opinions. Your goal in carrying out this assignment is to find out *why* your respondents like certain singers and recordings. It is not to find out what they listen to in an average day, though this information may be useful. Your concern is to get at the feelings people have for particular singers and recordings, to see what they "mean" to your respondents.

You will have to decide what this "meaning" is. People make all kinds of associations with singers and songs, and you should try to find out what these associations are for your respondents and what they signify. In essence, you will be fishing around, trying to find out things that your respondents themselves may not be aware of. Interview four to six people for this exercise, and spend approximately 20 minutes with each person.

Carrying Out the Depth Interviews

1. If you can, make audiotapes of your interviews, so you have precise records of what was said. Also, take notes on important matters while you interview each person.

2. Be on the lookout for feelings, opinions, and attitudes that people have, even if they seem irrelevant or trivial. What might seem trivial at first may end up telling you a good deal. This means that when you conduct your interviews, you should ask questions that are open-ended and allow your respondents plenty of room to speculate, offer opinions, and so on.

3. Record some preliminary demographic information on your respondents, so you can see if any correlations can be drawn between particular characteristics—socioeconomic class, education, gender, or race, for example—and what you find. For this exercise, you should interview only people who fall into a certain category and are alike in some important respect. That means you have to figure out a way to find respondents who will have the attributes you want.

4. Make a preliminary list of some questions you might want to ask to get the interview off to a good start and to get the information you want. In *Psychiatric Interviewing: A Primer* (1988), Robert L. Leon points out that people wait for clues—both verbal and nonverbal—that tell them how to respond when they are being interviewed. "Doctors, as well as patients, give clues of which they are unaware" (p. 8), Leon notes. He then makes a distinction between directive and nondirective interviewing:

> We speak of two kinds of interviews, directive and nondirective. This refers to the interviewer's communications to the patient about how the interview will progress and whether the doctor or patient will determine what information will come from the interview. The terms "directive" and "nondirective" do not refer to the interview's purpose. Nondirective means allowing patients to open the interview, develop it, and proceed at their own pace. The doctor must let go yet still maintain control, which may sound paradoxical. (p. 17)

Leon's book is intended for psychiatrists, so we must substitute "interviewer" and "respondent" for "doctor" and "patient" here. The important thing is that you let those being interviewed tell you what's on their minds instead of falling into the mode of just answering questions that are asked of them. Leon makes a distinction between an interview and an interrogation (as conducted, say, by the police). When interviewing, then, you must learn how to be a good listener and to pick up on statements made and openings given you by the respondent. Ask questions that elicit further comments and opinions, and ask for explanations of statements your respondent makes. And don't interrupt a respondent who is telling you about his or her feelings and thoughts because you have some information you want to get.

Following are some of the kinds of questions you might want to consider using in your depth interview for this assignment, after you have broken the ice with your respondent and established rapport:

- What is your favorite kind of music?
- What is it you like about it?
- How long have you liked it? Did you like something else before?
- What performers/singers/groups do you like the best?
- What is it about them that you like?
- Do you have many of their albums? How many? Which ones?
- What is your favorite album now? Any idea why?
- Do you have a favorite song now?
- Do you know the lyrics of the song?
- What do the lyrics mean to you?
- Is there anything special about the performance?
- How do you decide whether or not to buy an album?
- What albums have you bought recently?
- How often do you play them?
- What kinds of feelings do you get when you listen to your favorite singer/song/album?
- Do you tend to listen to your favorite singer/song/album at particular times, when you're in particular moods? If so, how would you describe those moods?
- Does the singer/song/album help you deal with any problems you have? If so, how?
- Do you ever buy albums because your friends do?
- Do you belong to any fan clubs? If so, for whom? If you were to join a fan club, which one would you join?
- What do you think is the most important thing about a song—the lyrics, the beat, the melody? Something else?
- If you could be switched into the body of some singer, which one would you choose?
- Have you ever been to any live performances in which you've seen singers or groups? If so, which ones? Which show did you like best?

- What's your favorite radio station? About how many hours a day/week do you listen to it? What kind of music does it play?

These are just some examples of the kinds of questions you might consider asking. It would not be a good idea to bring such a list of questions to the interview and ask them, one after another, because that would turn the interview into a survey. However, you should think about what questions might lead your respondents to discuss their preferences in some detail.

As the interviewer, you can interact with your respondent in a number of different ways as the interview progresses:

- *Understanding response:* Here you try to find out whether you understand what the respondent is telling you. You might ask for clarification of some kind. It is often useful to repeat something the interviewee has said in your question—"Did I understand you to say ... ?"
- *Probing response:* Here you try to obtain more information by asking follow-up questions and trying to get the respondent to discuss some point in more detail. You might ask how he or she feels about something, why he or she believes something, and so on.
- *Evaluative response:* Here you offer a judgment of some kind about what your respondent has told you. In conducting your depth interviews, you should take care to avoid such responses, because your purpose is to obtain information, not to render judgments.
- *Phatic response:* Here you just say something like "uh huh" to indicate that you have heard the respondent and wish him or her to continue. This is a form of feedback that helps keep the interview moving. Conversations are actually structured, and respondents need to know that you have heard them and that they can continue talking.

5. Be neutral. In conducting your interviews, you should not offer any of your own opinions, because they might affect the answers you get. Don't evaluate your respondents' statements, and don't offer your own opinions. And don't ask leading questions, questions that give respondents hints about the answers you are looking for. Your job, remember, is to keep your respondents talking about themselves— about their feelings, attitudes, and the like. You want to keep the conversation going and guide it, in as subtle a manner as possible, in the direction of the subject at hand. Say as little as possible, and when you do speak, do so only to obtain more information.

*Writing a Report on Your Depth Interviews*

1. Begin your report with an introductory paragraph or two on the subject of your depth interview and why it is interesting and important.

2. Describe your findings. What conclusions did you arrive at after your depth interviews? Were you able to discover anything interesting? Did your interviewees have any preferences in common? Did they use music in similar or different ways? Did you gain any insights (which we will define as the discovery of interesting relationships between phenomena not previously known) from the interviews? Did you find anything that suggests that further research would be profitable?

3. If you have found anything that you think is interesting, use quotations and paraphrases from your interviews to support your contentions. It is always better to *show* results to your readers (using quotations) than simply to tell them, especially if you have material that reveals hidden feelings and attitudes.

It may be, of course, that you discovered nothing interesting in your interviews. If that is the case, you should say so. You should not expect that research projects will always work out the way you hope or believe they will.

4. Discuss the problems you faced in doing this research project and tell how you tried to overcome them. You might also offer suggestions for carrying out such a study should someone else wish to repeat your research. Frequently, social scientists repeat research projects that have been done by other social scientists (a process known as replication) to see whether or not they get the same results.

5. Attach notes from your interviews to your report. Depth interviews are difficult in the sense that you don't know what you are looking for when you conduct them, and sometimes you don't know what you've found, either. But if it is true that people often act on the bases of attitudes, beliefs, and impulses of which they are unaware, depth interviews have a utility that makes them worth doing.

Aristotle argues that there are three kinds of rhetorical proof; that is, three ways in which a speaker can persuade an audience of his position—ethos, pathos, and logos. Ethos is ethical proof, the convincing character of the speaker. . . . Pathos is an appeal to the emotions of the audience. . . . Logos is logical proof, or argument, the kind of proof that appeals to reason. . . . Our sense of these elements will change according to at least two other primary factors, which are tightly related and which have to do with the nature of the specific discourse. Aristotle's breakdown of the kinds of rhetoric into legislative, judicial, and ceremonial is an acknowledgment that the aim of the discourse will determine the form in which it is expressed.

Robert L. Root, Jr., **The Rhetorics of Popular Culture: Advertising, Advocacy, and Entertainment** (1987, pp. 16-18)

# Chapter 7

## Rhetorical Analysis: Magazine Advertisements

Rhetoric is conventionally defined as the study of persuasion. Aristotle wrote a book titled *Rhetoric* in which this definition appears:

> Rhetoric may be defined as the faculty of observing in any given case the available means of persuasion. This is not the function of any other art. Every other art can instruct or persuade about its own particular subject-matter; for instance, medicine about what is healthy and unhealthy. . . . But rhetoric we look upon as the power of observing the means of persuasion on almost any subject presented to us. (Aristotle, 1941, p. 1329)

Rhetoricians typically analyze speech and written language, but the concept can also be extended to visual language; it is this expanded understanding of rhetoric that you will apply to the research project presented in this chapter.

You will investigate how magazine advertisements persuade people to purchase products or services. This means that you will try to determine how the copywriters and artists who work for advertising agencies use language and images to make magazine advertisements that they believe will "sell."

### Problems Faced in Making Rhetorical Analyses

In conducting a rhetorical analysis, the issue arises of whether rhetorical principles are being applied correctly. It is one thing to have a list of rhetorical principles (they follow shortly) and another to use those principles in the right way to try to detect the ways copywriters and artists attempt to convince us to purchase given products or services.

There is also the matter of which rhetorical principles are best applied to given advertisements, and whether there are nonrhetorical methods of analysis that would be more suitable. The answer to this second point is that many different techniques can be used to analyze any text (a term that scholars use to describe many kinds of works, including print ads, commercials, films, television shows, stories, songs, and books), and that rhetorical analysis is an appropriate method to try—especially when the issue of persuasion is important.

### Advantages of Rhetorical Analysis

Magazine advertisements have been chosen for this exercise in rhetorical analysis because they are easy to obtain and to study. Most families subscribe to magazines that are full of advertisements—often there are more pages devoted to advertisements than to editorial copy. Most magazines are targeted toward certain audiences, so we can often gain insights into these audiences by analyzing the advertisements and seeing how the people in the advertising agencies (who have studied these market segments extensively) view them.

Print advertisements are also easier to analyze than other kinds of advertising—radio or television commercials, for instance. Magazine advertisements contain language and images that stay put and can be studied without having to be transcribed.

Rhetoric is an ancient and complex subject, but a brief explanation of some of the basic modes of persuasion should enable you to make interesting and perceptive analyses. We all are exposed to many print advertisements during the course of any given day (in newspapers and magazines, on billboards). Quite likely you have thought about some of the print advertisements you have seen—ones that somehow caught your attention. This curiosity factor may help to motivate you to examine these advertisements more carefully and see how they work.

## Disadvantages of Rhetorical Analysis

We sometimes assume that by analyzing the techniques used to make advertisements persuasive, we can gain some insight into the intended audiences of the advertisements. But we must remember that in order for this to be so, the people who work for advertising agencies must have correct insights into the segments of the market they are targeting with their ads. Advertisers are not always correct, however, and many advertising campaigns are failures. We need to be careful about making generalizations concerning particular kinds or types of people and the most effective means that can be used to persuade them.

In the past, it was often assumed also that all people would interpret particular advertisements in more or less the same way. We now understand that this is not the case; different people have different personalities, educations, interests, values, and beliefs, and they see advertisements (and other texts) in many different ways. Umberto Eco, an Italian scholar (and novelist), argues that "aberrant decoding" often occurs when people are exposed to mass media. This is because of differences between the people who make the advertisements (and encode them in certain very specific ways) and the members of the audience (who decode them in a wide variety of ways). A copywriter, for example, may allude in an ad's copy to a famous work of art or literature, on the assumption that everyone who views the ad will be familiar with the work. People who don't know the work will probably not interpret the advertisement correctly.

## Rhetorical Analysis Project: A Magazine Advertisement

In this project you will study a magazine advertisement. You will use some of the more common principles of rhetorical analysis to see how images and other visual phenomena (such as type styles) and language in the advertisement have been used to shape a desired response—most typically some kind of persuasion. The desired response may be for readers of the ad to remember the name of the product, to consider using it or trying it at a later date, or to feel that they must purchase the product (or service) advertised immediately—by calling a toll-free telephone number, for instance.

## Rhetorical Devices Used in Persuasion

In studying your magazine advertisement, you will find it wise to keep in mind a point made by Tony Schwartz in his book *The Responsive Chord* (1974):

> The critical task is to design our package of stimuli so that it resonates with information already stored with the individual and thereby induces the desired learning or behavioral effect. Resonance takes place when the stimuli put into our communication evoke *meaning* in a listener or viewer. That which we put into the communication has no meaning in itself. The meaning of our communication is what a listener or viewer gets *out* of his experience with the communicator's stimulus. (pp. 24-25)

It is much easier to activate impulses and desires in individuals than to convince those individuals starting from scratch. So, in effect, advertisements attempt to "push our buttons." (In this chapter, I use the term *advertisement* only for print media advertising, and *commercial* for ads on radio and television.) They are stimuli designed to evoke appropriate responses, and we are what might be described as "complicated rats" who participate in the advertisers' experiments.

### Metaphoric Language

Metaphoric language communicates through analogy and compares two things. There are two forms of metaphoric language. In a *metaphor*, the analogy is direct: My love *is* a red rose. In a *simile*, the analogy is indirect: My love *is like* a red rose. Sometimes metaphors are found in a sentence's verbs, which suggest the comparison to be made: I *raced*; I *flew*; I *glided*.

## Metonymic Language

Metonymic language communicates by association and suggests that something is connected to something else. There are two forms. A *metonym* is a general association: A bowler hat (derby) suggests England. In a *synecdoche,* a part stands for the whole, or vice versa: The White House stands for the American presidency. We learn to make many such associations as we grow up; in U.S. society some common associations include the following:

> big houses and wealth
> dark shadows and horror
> BMWs and yuppies
> France and romance
> nature and innocence

Clearly we could add to this list almost endlessly. This means that copywriters and art directors in the United States can work with a repertoire of associations that they assume most Americans hold. Advertisements are full of metaphoric and metonymic devices—analogies and associations. If you find any in the advertisement you are studying, you should analyze them and consider how they are used.

## Verbal Appeals

There are a number of verbal appeals and approaches used commonly in advertising; these include solving a problem, offering expert advice, and using comparisons.

*Solving a problem.* Advertisements often pose problems (a beautiful woman has no boyfriends because her underarms smell) that they then solve (use Zilch underarm deodorant and find the man of your dreams). In some cases, copywriters create pseudoproblems or magnify trivial ones. They also play upon anxieties that many people have.

*Offering expert advice.* Copywriters sometimes play upon the common human need for reassurance by offering "experts" to give us advice. "More doctors recommend . . . ," they tell us. Sometimes ad-

vertisements present "experts" who are not really experts in the areas
in which they are offering advice.

*Using comparisons.* Often two products are compared, sometimes
in a variety of ways, to show that one product is superior to the other.
This is common in advertisements for cars, computers, and other kinds
of complicated machines and devices. This kind of approach is a direct
appeal to logic and rationality, but it is sometimes the case that the
product's most important aspects are not considered.

## Sexuality

Advertisers use sexuality in a number of different ways and for a
variety of purposes. One thing they do is play upon our desires for
sexual relationships by using images of attractive women (and, lately,
men) and suggestive language in advertisements that are designed to
arouse us sexually. Women are shown in various stages of undress or
using suggestive body language or in scenarios in which sexual activity (in the past or forthcoming) is implied—and this is often reinforced
by the language used, which is highly eroticized.

Sometimes, on the other hand, advertisers attempt to create anxieties in our minds about our sexuality and desirability, which they then
"solve" by suggesting products or services for us to use.

Advertisers use sexuality in an attempt to evade rationality (behavior dominated by the ego) and provoke emotional, impulsive acts
or decisions (behavior dominated by the id).

## Fears and Anxieties

Advertisers often try to appeal to us by targeting common fears
and anxieties. A distinction can be made between anxieties (which are
vague and don't have specific objects) and fears (which are much more
concrete and specific). Generally speaking:

We fear rejection by others.
We fear being lonely.
We fear being unloved.
We fear being different, standing out.

Not everyone has these particular fears, of course, but they tend to be common to many of us. We are social animals, and we tend to take comfort in being with others who are like us in one way or another.

Anxieties are much harder to pin down than fears—they are vague, diffuse feelings we sometimes have that plague us. But we can't locate any specific reason for having a given anxiety. We don't generally seem to enjoy being in a state of anxiety, and if we can find a way to escape it, so the logic goes, we will do so.

### The Herd Mentality

One way to convince people to buy something is to suggest that "everyone is doing it" and rely on the "herd mentality" in many people, who find safety in numbers. There are, of course, some people who see themselves as individualists and who resist such appeals.

### Desire for Approval

Advertisements that take advantage of our desire for the approval of others attempt to convince us that purchasing particular products or services will earn us the approval of those who are members of the "elite" or who are "in the know." Most people want to be approved of by others, and purchasing the right product is posited as a means of obtaining this approval.

### Keeping Up With the Joneses

Advertisers often assume that we want to show the world that we are successful and can keep up with others—which means purchasing the kinds of products and doing the kinds of things (taking expensive vacations, sending our kids to the right private schools, driving the right kind of car) that others do. Thorstein Veblen, a famous economics thinker, suggested that "conspicuous display" is a powerful force in human behavior, and keeping up with the Joneses means purchasing products that demonstrate we are successful.

### Imitation of Stars and Celebrities

Although we cannot have the "exciting" and "glamorous" lives that entertainment figures and celebrities have (or tell us they have), we can, at least, use many of the same products they use and that they peddle on television and radio. By doing so, we attain a kind of symbolic identification with them and their lifestyles. This "imitation" can also apply to the heroes and heroines they portray in films and television shows.

We identify with celebrities, heroes, and heroines at different stages of our lives and to varying degrees. Advertisers use this process of identification, which can be very powerful, to sell products.

### Reward Yourself

Certain advertisers tell us, indirectly and in a subtle manner, to "reward" ourselves by using their products. "You deserve it," they tell us, as payment for your hard work, your diligence, or whatever. The push is for immediate gratification and pleasure without regard for anything else.

### Stimulate Fantasy

Perfume advertisements are excellent examples of the use of fantasy (as well as the desire for sexual gratification) to sell a product. The language tends to be poetic and dreamy and is meant to generate fantasies and daydreams, often of an erotic nature. The product becomes identified with the fantasy. This fantasy is generated by the use of many verbal techniques associated with poetry: alliteration, repetition, rhyme, and highly metaphoric language. This kind of writing is best described as "pseudopoetic," given that it is created for commercial purposes.

### Slogans and Jingles

Jingles are catchy melodies that are designed to become embedded in our minds. They usually have a strong beat and clever use of language as well and are quite common in radio and television commercials. Slogans are phrases that describe products or the corporations that manufacture products. These phrases become identified with their products or corporations—they may be thought of as verbalized logos. Slogans are repeated over and over in advertisements, often appearing in particular typefaces to facilitate recognition. Sometimes a slogan is used as part of a jingle, which further facilitates recognition and memorableness.

## A Note on Oppositions

Concepts are based on oppositions; thus many of the appeals discussed above can be seen as representing one side of a set of paired opposites. For example:

envy/emulation
anxiety/security
rejection/acceptance
lack/satisfaction
individual/herd mentality
loneliness/popularity

When you look for verbal appeals in magazine advertisements, you should be mindful of the oppositions that are stated or implied in the language.

## Images and Visual Phenomena

The images, typefaces, colors, and other visual phenomena in advertisements also play particular roles in "selling" people on products and services.

*Balance.* In this context, *balance* refers to the physical arrangement of elements in an advertisement. There are two kinds of balance in advertisements: (a) *axial or formal balance,* in which the visual elements are balanced on either side of an imaginary vertical or horizontal line through the center of the advertisement; and (b) *dynamic or informal balance,* in which the visual elements are not arranged in a formal or balanced manner. Generally speaking, we associate formal balance, which has a static quality about it, with sophistication, elegance, and understatement. Most of the time in advertisements we find informal balance, which tends to be more visually exciting.

*Spatiality.* In the context of advertising, *spatiality* refers to the amount of white or empty space in an advertisement. We usually equate white space with sophistication and elite taste. Consider the difference, for example, between a newspaper advertisement for a supermarket, in which there is no white space, and a magazine advertisement for perfume or an expensive watch, which may be full of white space.

*Typefaces.* Different typefaces can suggest various things; each face has its own personality. Thin, elegant typefaces generate one kind of feeling, and thick, heavy typefaces generate another. There are hundreds of different typefaces and many sizes of each face. In thinking about the typefaces used in an advertisement, consider the product, its potential market, the lifestyles and tastes of people in this market, and the appropriateness of the typefaces used. Remember that conscious decisions have been made, usually by a typographer, regarding every typeface used and about the size of the typeface and the amount of space between lines of type.

*Color.* What colors are used in the advertisement and what significance do they have? Is the coloration bright or subdued? What might that mean? Does the coloration suggest sophistication and restraint, or passion and raw energy? Is color being used in a realistic fashion, or to stylize the product in some way?

*Camera shots and angles.* If there is a photographic image in the advertisement, what kind of camera shot is involved? If there are a number of photographic images, what are they like and why were they chosen? Do we look down on some scenario or do we look up at one? Is the shot a close-up or an extreme long shot? Are we level with the action? Why were the particular camera shot and angle chosen?

*Models.* There are a number of things to consider concerning the appearance of human beings, animals, and other models in advertisements:

- *gender:* male or female
- *age:* young, old, middle-aged
- *facial characteristics:* regularity of features, color of hair and eyes, complexion of skin, and so on
- *facial expressions:* emotions shown
- *body language:* attitudes shown by posture, position of limbs, and the like
- *lifestyle props:* hairstyles, clothes worn, eyeglass styles, and so on
- *relationships implied:* by scenario, language in copy

## Carrying Out a Rhetorical Analysis
## of a Magazine Advertisement

1. You should select a magazine advertisement that has an image and a substantial amount of printed matter (copy). It is hard to analyze persuasive techniques used in an advertisement that has only a few words of copy.

2. You should also select an advertisement that is visually interesting, so that you can examine the ways images and other visual materials are used to support the verbal material.

3. Use the list of rhetorical (persuasive) devices discussed above to analyze your text.

### Writing Up Your Rhetorical Analysis

1. Begin your write-up with an introduction in which you give the reader a general overview of what you are doing—making a rhetorical analysis of a magazine advertisement in terms of the language and visual elements found in it. It would be useful to say something about the nature of rhetorical analysis and the way you are using it. Attach

the advertisement to your paper, so the reader can see what you are discussing.

2. Tell the reader what interesting things you found in the advertisement, referring to such things as the copy (language) and visual elements. You probably will want to discuss specific aspects of the language and the visual devices used. Make sure you support your contentions with evidence that a reasonable person might find persuasive. That is, you should have some reasons or justifications for the points you make. In the case of your analysis of the language, for example, you should tie some rhetorical concept to your point.

If you consulted any books on rhetorical analysis or on advertising, you can make use of any information you found in those works by relating it to your analysis. Even though you might not have found an analysis of the particular advertisements you were investigating, you can discuss information about advertising, images, and other related concerns that applies to your research.

3. Discuss any interesting insights or conclusions that stem from your research. Did your research help you discover something you consider important? Did you gain any insights from the research?

4. Discuss any important problems you encountered in doing this research and any qualifications you wish to make about your findings or any generalizations you made based on your findings. (Remember, it is a good idea to qualify your generalizations and to avoid making extreme *all* or *every* statements.)

An important part of the preparation for research work consists in learning how to use the resources of libraries. It is important because all research inevitably involves the use of the book, pamphlet, periodical, and documentary materials in libraries. This applies to studies based on original data gathered in a field study as well as those based entirely upon documentary sources. In both types of studies there is the same need for using certain basic kinds of published materials. On the one hand, general source materials have to be consulted for the necessary background knowledge of the problem to be investigated. Obviously, no research project can be undertaken without this preliminary orientation. Nor should one be undertaken without knowledge of the research that has already been done in the field. It provides further orientation to the problem, and at the same time eliminates the possibility of unnecessary duplication of effort. In addition, valuable information on research techniques may be gained from reports of previous research.

Joseph S. Komidar, "The Uses of the Library," in William J. Goode and Paul K. Hatt (Eds.), **Methods in Social Research** (1952, p. 103)

# Chapter 8

## Library Research: Audiences of Radio Talk Shows

Searching in a library for information on a particular subject can be very much like looking for a needle in a haystack, especially if you don't know how to conduct your search. One of the more important parts of the librarian's job nowadays is *information retrieval*—that is, finding needed information using the library's resources. Many major university libraries have millions of books, plus magazines, newspapers, and all kinds of other documents (often in many different languages as well), and new material is coming in all the time. Thousands of new books are published every year in the United States, as well as seemingly countless numbers of scholarly journals, popular magazines, and government reports.

Librarians often face formidable problems in determining where to put what. For example, suppose a book is published that is a history of political philosophy. Does the book go in the history section, the political science section, or the philosophy section of the library? Fortunately, this is a problem for catalogers, not for us. What is important for library users is the ability to find a particular book or information on a particular topic when they need it.

The purpose of the library search, in the context of this chapter's exercise, is to obtain enough relevant information from experts and other reliable sources to help answer some question. Typically, when a student writes a term paper, he or she tries to find quotations from experts and other authorities (relevant sources) that are related to the topics of the student's report. The student gathers material and then assembles it into an argument, using quotations from the experts to support his or her position and the conclusion the student has reached.

You do research because you want to know something. In some cases, you can never find an answer that everyone will accept. For example, suppose you want to prove that the San Francisco 49ers are the greatest football team of all time. You can assemble data, statistics, and so on, but this is a topic that can never be resolved, because there are no generally accepted criteria for proving something like this. There are other questions of a similar nature: Was Napoleon "good" or "bad"? What "caused" the Civil War? The important point here is that some questions can never be answered in ways that will satisfy everyone, so you must be careful about the questions you ask and the problems you select for your research. "Why" questions and evaluative questions are difficult to address.

Suppose that you have an assignment to write a paper on some recent historical event, and you need to gather information. You can find, in the library, reports from eyewitnesses (in newspaper articles, books, diaries, journals, radio and television programs, and so on) as well as articles and books on the event by scholars (who, we presume, have conducted a variety of different kinds of research). You can then use the material you have gathered as "evidence" in your paper. You may paraphrase the authors of the material or you may quote them directly, but in all cases you must acknowledge where you got your information.

You use your evidence the way a prosecuting attorney uses witnesses in an attempt to convict a person who is accused of some crime. And, as in a trial, there may be conflicting reports by witnesses about what "really" happened. What do you do when "experts" and "authorities" disagree with one another, which is often the case? You have to decide which expert or authority is most credible, and why.

Sometimes just digging out facts can be quite a problem, and you may have assignments that ask nothing more of you than to get information about some topic. Generally, however, you will be asked to do more than find facts; you will be asked to assemble information that will support some kind of a thesis, some kind of a generalization.

## Problems in Doing Library Research

You may find it difficult to locate relevant sources of information on your subject of interest. What do you do if you can't find anything on your subject? How do you start searching for the information you need? You might begin by consulting some of the following sources:

- the library's card catalog (often on computer now)
- databases on various topics, often found in libraries
- encyclopedias and other reference works of various kinds
- indexes to periodicals, such as the *Readers' Guide to Periodical Literature, New York Times Index,* and *Book Review Digest*
- bibliographies devoted to specific topics
- textbooks and scholarly journals, which often have substantial bibliographies
- research librarians
- the popular media—newspapers, magazines, best-selling books, videos of news shows and television programs, and so on

You must get up-to-date information. You should try to get the most recent work on whatever topic it is you are researching. If all of your sources are 10 or 15 years old (in some cases, even a couple of years old), you will be downgraded for using "dated" material. Suppose you are doing a project on the Civil War. You would be perfectly correct to use material written by people who were in the war (diaries) and by people who observed it (newspaper reporters, historians of the time, and politicians), but you would also want to have the latest interpretations of modern-day historians, which you might find in scholarly journals.

Historians, remember, disagree on many things, because they interpret what went on in the past. They can't tell you what happened; rather, they make their own cases for what they think happened. This applies to scholars in other disciplines as well.

## Advantages of Library Searches

Library searches don't cost anything if you do them yourself. If you use a computer and do a search using a database, there may be a charge for the service—sometimes such costs are considerable. But if you use your own resources and confine yourself to material in the card catalog of the library you are using, this kind of research costs nothing.

In doing library research you don't have the difficult problems that often come with "designing research," and you don't have to deal with people (as in depth interviews, surveys, or experiments). You don't have to worry about whether or not people will cooperate with you and be truthful. Your basic problem in library research lies in searching out the information that the library holds.

### Disadvantages of Library Searches

One fundamental problem of library research is that the material you get has usually been filtered through someone else's mind—that of some writer or photographer or editor. You are always dealing, in a sense, with secondhand information.

Sometimes a library won't have the books and periodicals you need, or you may find them listed in the library's catalog or indexes, but when you go to get them you discover that they have been checked out or lost (through misfiling or theft).

Despite these difficulties, libraries (especially university libraries) are remarkable institutions, and it is amazing how much material they have. Students are not the only people who do library research. Many people in the media and in various other professions use libraries to get the information they need.

For the project you are asked to do for this chapter, on talk shows, you will need a university library—one that has scholarly journals that deal with broadcasting, communications, popular culture, journalism, and the mass media. Public libraries—city and county libraries—often have many popular periodicals that have material on these subjects, but it is usually not material written by scholars, which is necessary for this exercise.

### Library Search Assignment: Audiences of Radio Talk Shows

For this exercise, you need to find the latest material on audiences of radio talk shows and on related topics such as the following:

- who listens to radio talk shows and, of related interest, any changes over the years in the demographics of audiences of radio talk shows

- the effects of these talk shows on people and on society
- why people listen (or say they listen) to radio talk shows

Obtain this material by finding research journals that deal with the mass media and related areas. You need to use research journals because generally they are more up-to-date than books. It usually takes more than a year to publish a book, whereas most journals appear quarterly or bimonthly; thus journals are the best place to find reports of the latest research.

Try to find as many scholarly sources as you can. You should also consult books that may have material on radio talk shows, to see whether the journal articles support what is in the books or have new findings that contradict or modify the books' information in some way.

A great deal of research has been done and is being done on radio talk shows, but most of it is proprietary—that is, it is paid for by radio stations, which will not, generally, share their findings with others. You may, however, be able to obtain some data about the popularity of various talk shows from public relations departments of radio stations and from broadcasting trade journals and reports published by ratings organizations. Also, some newspapers carry columns on radio that may be of use. Your main sources, however, should be research articles by scholars.

To summarize, you might find the material you are looking for in some of the following sources:

- books on the subject
- chapters on the subject within more general books
- scholarly articles in scholarly journals
- popular articles in magazines read by the general public; also articles in trade journals
- newspaper articles
- encyclopedia articles such as those found in the *Encyclopedia of Communication*, published by Oxford University Press
- abstracts of scholarly articles

In doing this research, you are working within a very large field called *communications*. You can narrow your search for information by considering the following:

- Communications is your general area.
- The mass media make up a subcategory of this area.
- Electronic media make up a subcategory of mass media.
- Broadcast media make up a subcategory of electronic media.
- Radio is a subcategory of electronic media.
- Talk shows are a genre or kind of program carried on radio.
- The audiences of talk shows make up a subject related to talk shows.

You may find material that is relevant in any area of this list of categories and subcategories. For example, some theories of communications may help explain why audiences of radio talk shows behave the way they do, so there are many different areas that you can investigate in looking for useful information on radio talk shows. Don't assume that you can use only articles on audiences of radio talk shows—though you certainly should have some research articles on them, as well as data about them.

### Writing Up Your Research Project

1. Begin with an introduction in which you give the reader some general background on your subject, an overview, a sense of context. You might give a brief history of the development of radio talk shows and say something about their importance before discussing the questions you investigated in doing your research.

2. Tell the reader what your research questions were and what your conclusions are. You should explain how you went about getting information, what you found, and how you arrived at your conclusions. If you found articles that contradicted each other on topics such as how many people listen to these shows, who listens, why they listen, and the effects of these shows on listeners and society in general, explain how you evaluated the conflicting material and why you came to the conclusions you did.

3. Provide the reader with data and other reasons to accept your conclusions. If you have to qualify your conclusions, explain why. If you had any difficulties in doing your research, explain what they were and how you dealt with them. In addition to discussing the problems

---

**Exhibit 8.1**

*How to Read Analytically*

1. *Look for important concepts and ideas* and how they are explained and used. For example, is the concept "materialism" used? If so, how is it defined and employed by the writer?
2. *Look for factual material, data, and statistics* that are used to support arguments.
3. *Look for arguments made by the author.* Why does the author believe or not believe something? What methodologies are employed?
4. *Look for contrasts and comparisons.* Frequently authors embed these in their texts. When you can, make a chart that shows these contrasts and comparisons.
5. *Look at the examples used.* Are they relevant? Do they support assertions? Or are they too selective, neglecting other examples that might not support these assertions?
6. *Look for threads,* topics that keep coming up repeatedly. What significance do these threads have?
7. *Look for insights*—this can be understood as seeing relationships between or among phenomena that you never saw before. Are these insights valuable? Where do they lead you?
8. *Don't expect to agree with everything an author writes.* If you disagree, make sure you have valid reasons. Even if authors are wrong about some things, they may be right about other things.
9. *Consider adaptations you can make.* For example, essays on the nature of heroes and heroines in Greek mythology can sometimes be applied to characters in the mass media in interesting ways. You may not be able to find an article on a particular situation comedy, but you may find material on situation comedies in general or on humor that you can apply.
10. *What about the author's style?* How important is style in convincing you to believe something? What is distinctive about the author's style?
11. *What sources does the author quote?* Do these sources give you any ideas about the author's point of view, politics, values, seriousness?

NOTE: You should keep these considerations in mind when you write, for readers will be using these analytic notions to interpret your papers.

---

you faced, offer suggestions for any researcher who may wish to undertake similar research.

4. Provide some kind of wrap-up at the end of your paper, so the reader isn't left hanging. There are several methods you can use. For example, you might summarize what you have found, so the reader gets a good general view of what you have done. Or you might discuss the implications of your work and, perhaps, provide a refinement of

the conclusion you stated earlier in your paper. Whatever the case, don't leave the reader hanging by stopping abruptly because, perhaps, you have reached the minimum number of pages required in your assignment.

If you were out in the so-called real world and had a job as a reporter for a newspaper or television station, you would employ the same techniques you will be using in carrying out this assignment. We live in an information age, as I've said before, and most people who work in the information society constantly find themselves searching for information on a wide variety of subjects.

Let me conclude by quoting the first paragraph of the first chapter of an excellent book, *Search Strategies in Mass Communication*, by Jean Ward and Kathleen A. Hansen (1987):

> The news assignment: an article or series of articles on gentrification, or the displacement of urban poor from old neighborhoods that are undergoing rehabilitation. The reporter: a generalist who must begin by recognizing her own lack of knowledge about this subject. The challenge: to do a rapid study of gentrification. The sources: knowledgeable people and reputable books and articles. In conducting her survey of what is known about the subject, the well-prepared reporter will range widely and consult experts in such fields as economics, architecture, insurance, banking, housing, city planning, demographics, race relations, urban affairs, and tax policy. Her choice of people to be interviewed will be influenced by what she learns in her overview of the subject. Her questions to interviewers will be shaped partly by a need to expand on and to update what she learns in her first study of the subject. (p. 1)

You will not be asked to interview people in this exercise, but you will be doing the same kind of thing the mythical reporter described above was asked to do.

Library searches are not make-work, designed by malicious professors interested only in making your life miserable. Learning to do library research will provide you with a tool that you can and will use in your career, for one of the most important things students can learn is how to continue learning, how to find information on subjects that interest them. There is now so much information available that nobody can keep up with it. What is important is being able to find information when you want it.

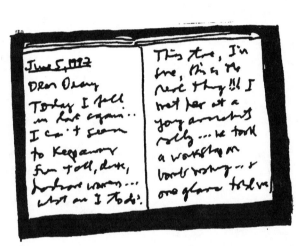

In late August and early September, with the story of John Zaccaro's finances dominating the news, the wounded Democratic campaign tested image and issues ads to use in the race against Reagan. The findings of focus groups conducted by Edward J. Reilly of Boston say a great deal about the problems Mondale faced and offer feedback concerning how a presidential campaign can evaluate its advertising effort. The lessons might equally apply to any candidate attempting to develop a coherent message after his or her credibility has been severely damaged.

In a series of "Mondale to Camera" ads tested on September 4, the Reilly group concluded that respondents were "distracted by the visuals and by his presence" and "had difficulty understanding the message" concerning education, taxes, and the deficit. Several remarked that Mondale might be right on the issues, but they didn't "see how he's going to do it." One undecided farmer reached the conclusion most feared by the Mondale campaign: "He reminds me of Carter in those ads."

Montague Kern, **30-Second Politics: Political Advertising in the Eighties** (1989, pp. 118-119)

# Chapter 9

## Focus Groups: Reasons for Attending Films

Focus groups are group interviews that are held to find out how people feel about some product, service, or issue. A group of people are assembled and a free-form discussion is held, led by a moderator, to obtain the desired information. As Roger D. Wimmer and Joseph R. Dominick describe it in *Mass Media Research: An Introduction* (1983), "The focus group technique involves interviewing two or more people simultaneously, with a moderator or facilitator leading the respondents in a relatively free discussion about the topic under consideration" (p. 100). Those who conduct focus groups are usually interested in people's attitudes and behaviors relative to some consumer product or choice (as in elections) they might make.

The aim of the focus group discussion is not to build consensus, but just the opposite—to find out what each member of the group thinks about the topic under discussion, and to elicit from each person his or her opinions and descriptions of the behavior of interest. Focus groups are, then, a method for probing to find out how people think and act. A focus group discussion is a kind of collective depth interview, conducted with the hope that it will lead to important insights that can help manufacturers of products or sellers of services function more efficiently.

### Problems With Focus Groups

The first problem in doing focus group research is that of getting a suitable group of people together to form the focus group. If you want to find out about how people respond to a new product that is being developed to compete with an established product, you must find people who use the product, or who might be persuaded to use it. In actuality, it is not too difficult to assemble focus groups. There are companies that have a good deal of expertise in assembling these groups and in running focus group interviews. Participants are often paid small sums to be part of focus groups and often find the experience rather pleasant, being with a group of people chatting about some topic and having their opinions count for something.

In this research technique, the ability of the moderator is crucial. A focus group moderator must not be directive or too assertive, but must also make sure the discussion doesn't get off track. As Ward and Hansen (1987) note:

> The moderator of a focus group lets the discussion range while it is moving productively and producing useful comment. Tasks include making certain that main points are covered, being receptive to new points that arise, and making sure that each respondent has a chance to talk. (p. 178)

Leading a discussion is often difficult. It takes a light touch and a good deal of skill to get everyone to contribute.

### Advantages of Focus Group Research

Focus groups are a relatively inexpensive way to do research. The moderator must be paid, and participants generally receive some small payment, but even so holding a focus group is still a great deal less expensive than conducting a survey. According to Wimmer and Dominick (1983), the price range can be from as little as a few hundred dollars to as high as several thousand dollars "depending on the size of the group, the difficulties in sample selection, and the company that conducts the group" (p. 101). Focus groups are often used in advertising and market research, and several thousand dollars is a relatively small percentage of the money that is spent on research and the production of advertising.

Focus groups can be assembled quickly, and the insights of the people who participate in focus groups are immediately available. Focus group sessions are often audiotaped and can also easily be videotaped, so that, in addition to their opinions, respondents' body language and other behaviors can be analyzed in some detail. Audiotaping and videotaping can be done unobtrusively.

Focus groups also provide a great degree of interviewing flexibility. The moderator can easily follow up on members' comments, ask questions as needed, solicit opinions, raise issues, and so on. He or she can follow chance leads and obtain valuable information firsthand.

Group dynamics work so that respondents often become caught up in the discussion and stimulate others to contribute, sometimes offering information that is very useful. In a group situation, inhibitions can often be overcome, and material buried in the psyche can be accessed.

## Disadvantages of Focus Group Research

Because of the nature of focus groups, there are problems with the generalizability of results. A focus group represents a relatively small group of people, and they may not be representative of the potential users of a product or service. That is why it is important to assemble focus groups carefully.

The data from focus groups do not lend themselves to quantification. Respondents state their opinions, display their attitudes, and provide their recollections of past behavior (which may be incorrect). These kinds of discussions can provide answers to "why" questions, but not "how many" questions, which is why some researchers think focus groups are primarily useful for making pilot studies or as a complement to other kinds of studies.

Some participants in focus groups tend to monopolize the conversation and must be restrained without inhibiting other members of the group. Conversely, some members of the group might be shy and have to be drawn out without being made uncomfortable.

Some focus group members may be inhibited by knowing that they are being tape-recorded (and video-recorded, if that is done). If audio- and/or videotaping is to take place, the group members must be told at the very beginning and must be asked to sign releases for the taping; it is extremely unethical to record people without their knowledge.

### Focus Group Project: How People
### Decide Which Films to Attend

In this project you will try to find out why people go to some films and not others—that is, what is most important in their decision making. You will limit your group to students and, to make things easier, take some already assembled group of students (such as a group of three or four people having lunch at the school cafeteria) to function as your ad hoc focus group. You could also use members of some club or other entity who would be willing to spend some time (perhaps a half hour).

Generally speaking, the moderator of a focus group has a list of subjects that he or she needs to guide the group to address. In the case of film choice, the following possibilities suggest themselves. The most important reason people go to a particular film might be one of the following:

1. the director
2. the stars
3. the genre
4. word of mouth
5. reviews
6. cheapest theater
7. nearest theater
8. went with friends who made choice

The function of the discussion is *not* to get members of the group to agree on one or more reasons, but to find out how or why each member decides to go to a film. Your concern should be with past behavior—why your respondents have acted in the ways they have in the past. But your respondents' opinions about why they think people decide to go to one film rather than another may also be useful.

### Suggestions for Moderators

Here are the procedures you should follow once you have found the group of people who will be functioning as your focus group:

1. Explain the purpose of the focus group—how focus groups work, what their function is, and so on. If possible, tape-record the discussion. Explain that you are recording the discussion so that you can quote

people accurately in the report you will be writing. If you don't have a tape recorder or access to one, take careful notes and do the best you can.

2. Make the members of the group feel at ease. Explain to them that nobody is wrong in focus groups, that all opinions are valuable.

3. Get any demographic information from your respondents that might be useful or interesting.

4. Don't direct the discussion, but draw people out, to the extent that you can.

5. Follow up on any leads you get. That is, if someone says something that you think is interesting and may have important implications, draw him or her out on the matter. And ask others for their comments on the subject.

6. Try to get everyone involved in the discussion; don't allow anyone to dominate or monopolize the conversation.

7. Make sure that the group sticks to the subject and doesn't go off on tangents. For instance, respondents might want to discuss the films they have just seen instead of why they chose to see these films; you must guard against the discussion going off track.

8. Repeat back to people occasionally what you understand them to have said, as a means of clarifying what they mean and perhaps stimulating others to contribute to the discussion.

9. At certain times, ask specific members of the group for their opinions, instead of making generalized requests ("Does anyone have an opinion on this?").

## Writing a Report on Your Focus Group Discussion

1. Begin your write-up with a brief introduction in which you describe the makeup of your focus group and discuss the topic you researched.

2. List and discuss, in order of importance, the reasons your respondents gave as being most important in their decisions about what movies to attend. Offer significant quotations and explain their importance.

3. Did you have any preliminary hypotheses in mind before you led the focus group? If so, what led you to these hypotheses? How do you feel about your hypotheses after leading the focus group?

4. What (if any) insights did you gain or unusual findings did you make as a result of conducting the focus group? What conclusions did you come to? Remember to qualify your generalizations, especially if your focus group was small and ad hoc (fashioned from what was immediately available).

5. Did you experience any difficulties in carrying out this project? If so, describe them.

Experimentation—the observation of phenomena under controlled conditions. In laboratory experiments the investigator himself creates the setting for his observations, where in field experiments he manipulates only some of the variables in an established social setting. A third category of natural experiments is sometimes used to refer to cases where the investigator actually controls nothing, but where events happen to occur in a way similar to that which an investigator might wish to create through controlled conditions.

James A. Schellenberg, **An Introduction to Social Psychology** (1974, p. 348)

# Chapter 10

## Experiments: Humor

We often read about interesting and ingenious experiments that researchers in various fields have carried on and about what they have discovered. This is because we are naturally curious about ourselves and others and find descriptions of experiments fascinating. Many of the experiments that we read about in magazines and newspapers or hear about on radio and television have been conducted in the fields of medicine and other physical sciences. But there are also many interesting experiments done by social scientists that make the news.

### What Is an Experiment?

An experiment, for our purposes, will be understood to be a kind of a test that is held to do one of the following things:

- demonstrate that a proposition is true
- examine the validity of a hypothesis
- discover something that is not known or the utility of something that has not been tried before

In the first case, we experiment to prove that what is held to be true about a proposition actually is true. In some cases we replicate (repeat) experiments that have already been conducted to make certain that their findings are correct.

In the second case, we experiment to show that some hypothesis we have about some proposition or phenomenon is correct. A hypothesis can be defined as a statement about a relationship between phenomena that can be tested empirically. For example, as a result of doing some research on violence in society we might hypothesize that increased exposure to violence in the media leads to increased violence in the behavior of children and adolescents. Experiments have to be devised to determine whether this hypothesis is correct or not.

In the third case, we experiment to discover something that we did not already know or the utility of something that has not been tried before. For example, we might wonder whether a certain medicine, devised for one illness, would be useful in helping people with a different illness.

As John Brewer and Albert Hunter write in *Multimethod Research: A Synthesis of Styles* (1989):

> Experimentation, more than other styles of research, promises clear causal inferences. Its strategy is to manipulate exposure to an hypothesized cause, while controlling for the contaminating influence of other possible causes by the use of control groups and by the random assignment of subjects to control and experimental situations. (p. 47)

The purpose of the experiment is to make sure that the findings are valid and that the observed effects on the experimental group are not the result of some unknown influence that is the true cause of differences found between the experimental group and the control group.

Thus in an experiment, subjects are divided into two groups: a control group and an experimental group. Assignment of subjects to these groups should be random. The question then is, Has what the experimental group been exposed to actually led to the effects that have been found? Let me offer an example. Suppose that a researcher wants to see whether exposure to comic violence in films leads to increased violence in young children when they play. The researcher takes a grade school class and randomly divides the students into two groups: A (control) and B (experimental). The researcher then separates the two groups; the members of Group A read quietly, while the members of Group B are exposed to a film containing comic violence. Then the researcher observed both groups at play and counts the numbers of acts of violence displayed by members of Group A and Group B.

If there is a great deal more violence in Group B than in Group A, the researcher can hypothesize that exposure to comic violence leads to increased violence in young children. This might appear to be simple, but because human beings are so complicated, there are always problems in designing experiments, conducting them, and generalizing from the results.

## Advantages of Experiments

The basic advantage of an experiment is that, if carried out correctly, it can provide very strong evidence that the independent variable (such as the exposure of the experimental group to comic violence) actually has the effect it is thought or hypothesized to have, and that the effect discovered is not the result of some other unrecognized or unanticipated factor. Experiments also provide ways of discovering information and new relationships among phenomena that were previously unexpected or unrecognized.

We use the term *serendipity* to describe surprises and accidents that turn out to be significant. Sometimes, researchers conducting experiments on particular phenomena, especially in the physical sciences, have lucky accidents that lead them to discover other things, sometimes things that are of greater importance than what they were originally investigating.

## Disadvantages of Experiments

One big problem with experiments (of the nature we are concerned with here) is that they are artificial. When people know that they are involved in an experiment, this may affect their behavior. Further, the designs of many experiments suggest strong cause-and-effect relationships between the phenomena being investigated. Thus experimental findings may overstate cause-and-effect relationships, oversimplifying complex matters.

Experiments may also sometimes be harmful to the subjects involved in them. The late social psychologist Stanley Milgram did some research in the 1960s (his so-called Eichmann experiment) that was so disturbing to participants that many of them later needed therapy; as a result of this research, stringent controls are now required for experiments involving human beings. (Strictly speaking, one could argue that Milgram's study did not constitute an experiment, because he did not use a control group. Deciding what is and isn't a true experiment is sometimes difficult.) Milgram (1965) has described his research as follows:

> Two persons arrive at a campus laboratory to take part in a study of memory and learning. (One of them is a confederate of the experimenter.) Each subject is paid $4.50 upon arrival and is told that payment is not affected in any way by performance. The experimenter provides an introductory talk on memory and learning processes and then informs the subjects that in the experiment one of them will serve as teacher and the other as learner. A rigged drawing is held so that the naive subject is always assigned the role of teacher and the accomplice becomes the learner. The learner is taken to an adjacent room and is strapped into an electric chair.
>
> The naive subject is told that it is his task to teach the learner a list of paired associates, to test him on the list, and to administer punishment whenever the learner errs in the test. Punishment takes the form of electric shock, delivered to the learner by means of a shock generator controlled by the naive subject. The teacher is instructed to increase the intensity of the electric shock one step on the generator for each error. The generator contains 30 voltage levels ranging from 15 to 450 volts, and verbal designations ranging from "Slight Shock" to "Danger: Severe Shock." The learner, according to plan, provides many wrong answers, so that before long the naive subject must give him the strongest shock of the generator. Increases in shock levels are met by increasingly insistent demands from the learner that the experiment be stopped because of growing discomfort to him. However, the experimenter instructs the teacher to continue with the procedure and disregard the learner's protests. (p. 128)

Milgram gave lectures on his controversial research at which he displayed photographs of his subjects that showed the incredible amount of strain on their faces as many of them proceeded (so they thought) to shock the person strapped into the electric chair. He was studying obedience, and he designed his experiment to find out the degree to which people would be obedient in a difficult situation.

Milgram, who was a personal friend of mine, told me that he had asked many deans of schools of social and behavioral science how far they thought naive subjects would go in administering shocks, and most of the deans said they doubted that people would go beyond the third level. To Milgram's surprise, a considerable number of his subjects obeyed instructions to the extent of administering the most severe shock on their supposedly shock-generating consoles.

## An Experimental Research Project

In this experiment you will test the impact of people's previous exposure to humor on their assessment of a humorous television program or film. Your hypothesis: There is reason to believe that people who are exposed to some form of humor (such as jokes or cartoons) before viewing a humorous television program or film will be aroused by the first form of humor and will thus evaluate the television program or film as more humorous than will people in a control group that is not exposed to the first form of humor.

### Carrying Out a Simple Experiment

It is difficult to carry out experiments under the best conditions, so this little exercise will be somewhat simplified in nature. However, it does contain the basic elements of an experiment as discussed above.

1. Invite 10 friends to your home to carry out this experiment. To the extent that you can arrange it, the people you invite should be similar in many characteristics: age, gender, education, and so on.
2. Write the numbers 1 through 10 on slips of paper and put the slips in a paper bag. Have your friends draw numbers from the bag; assign those who draw odd numbers to your control group and those who draw even numbers to your experimental group.
3. Separate the control and experimental groups into two rooms. Have the experimental group members read a collection of jokes and cartoons or listen to a comedy recording of some kind. Have the control group members listen to nonhumorous recordings or view a nonhumorous short documentary.
4. After 15 minutes, bring the two groups together and show them a humorous situation comedy or a short comedy film.
5. Have everyone assess the film using the following questions:

    On a scale of 1-10, with 10 being funniest, how funny (in general) was the television show/film you just saw?

    How many funny gags or scenes do you remember?

6. Have each participant indicate whether he or she had an odd or an even number—that is, whether he or she was in the control group or the experimental group.

7. Compare the evaluations made by the members of the control group and the experimental group. If the members of the experimental group give the television show/film higher numbers than do the control group members, the hypothesis stated above is supported.

### Writing a Report on Your Experiment

1. Begin your write-up by describing what you did in detail. Tell the reader what humor your experimental group was exposed to, describe the age and gender makeup of the members of each group, and provide other relevant demographic data.

2. "Massage" your data. That is, tell what you found when you checked over the responses of your experimental and control groups (a) in general, (b) according to gender, (c) according to age, and (d) in any other ways. Do your data support the hypothesis that previous exposure to humor tends to make people more responsive to humor? Explain your answer.

3. Discuss any problems you had in carrying out this experiment and what you did to overcome them. Did everyone you invited show up? If not, what did you do? How does the number of people involved in the experiment affect your ability to make generalizations? Did some kind of a "crowd enhancement" effect play any role in the opinions of the members of the two groups? What changes can you think of that would improve the experiment?

As for the term "participant observation," it is a misnomer. The scientist . . . must always be able to take the role of his subjects, to participate symbolically, if he is to interpret or impute meaning to the actions of others. "Participant observation," as the term is usually employed, simply means the researcher engages in the activities of the group under study. He attends church, participates in festivals, drinks with the boys, or whatever. . . .

But there are liabilities to any effort to maximize one's immersion in a system. Aside from the danger of losing one's identity as a scientist, the researcher may become the captive of the group he is studying. His observations may no longer represent his independent judgments or evaluations but may reflect the observer's definition of the situation. For there is more to observation than simply taking the role of the other: The scientist must remain free to make interpretative judgments. Although some studies of small groups warn against the distortions in the observer's perception that result from social pressures, few, if any, authors point to the misperceptions that result from social controls exerted by the group under investigation.

Gideon Sjoberg and Roger Nett,
**A Methodology for Social Research** (1968, p. 176)

# Chapter 11

## Participant Observation:
## Video Game Players

*Participant observation* means just what it says. The researcher participates (to varying degrees) in some activity in order to observe and
better understand those involved in the activity. Participant observation thus is a kind of fieldwork an investigator does to gain insight into
some subculture or organization or activity of interest. For example,
participant observation studies have been made of hospital emergency
rooms, jails, drug addicts, and medical schools. The investigators'
purposes in conducting these observations are to find out what goes
on in the subcultures or organizations being studied and to gain some
insight into their operations (especially hidden aspects not easily rec-
ognized) and how they function. As Brewer and Hunter (1989) note:

> Fieldwork promises realistic theories that do justice to the complexity
> of actual social life. It is distinguished from other styles of research
> by the fact that the fieldworker personally enters natural social
> groups and studies them, as far as possible, in their full and natural
> state. . . . Most field research focuses on only one or a few groups, or
> upon a relatively small sample of individuals. This frees resources
> and also allows fieldworkers to develop not only an inside knowl-
> edge of the group but also the necessary rapport with subjects to
> conduct intensive multifaceted studies. However, this small scale
> also leads to questions about the representativeness of fieldwork's
> findings. . . . Participant observation obviously has its limitations,
> but it also is fascinating and sometimes leads to extremely interesting
> insights about members of the groups being observed. (pp. 45-46)

## An Example of a Possible
## Participant Observation Study

Let's take gymnasiums, or health clubs, as an example. Suppose that the aim of the participant observer is to find out "what goes on" in the health club. Who belongs? Why do they belong? What are the rites and rituals involved? What do the people who join the health club believe? How do members use the health club? What functions does being a member of the health club serve (both manifest or intended and latent or unintended)?

The manifest functions of belonging to a health club are to get exercise and improve one's physical health, but there are also unrecognized (in many cases) latent functions, such as to find suitable sexual partners and to take care of narcissistic needs (looking at one's body or muscles in the mirrors).

Participant observers must make certain they maintain their objectivity and don't "go native"—that is, without being aware of what they are doing, adopt the beliefs and values of the group they are studying (this has been known to happen). They also have to avoid changing the natural dynamics of the group they are studying, so doing participant observation poses certain tactical problems for researchers. For example, one has to be unobtrusive (to the extent possible) yet also do things like taking notes, counting, and writing down important statements made by various individuals in the group being studied.

Following are some of the concerns that face the participant observer:

1. How do you obtain focus? That is, what is to be observed?
2. How do you record your observations without changing the natural dynamics of what you are observing?
3. How do you make sure your notes and records are accurate? (How do you make sure that you distinguish between *descriptions* of events that took place and your *interpretations* of those events?)
4. How do you relate to those being observed (and get desired information) and still maintain objectivity?
5. How much can you generalize from your observations? How do you need to qualify your generalizations?

In participant observation, the researcher spends time observing people who are in some ways different from him- or herself. It is a form of ethnography carried out in one's own society, rather than in some distant land. As James Spradley notes in *The Ethnographic Interview* (1979):

> The essential core of this activity aims to understand another way of life from the native point of view. . . . Fieldwork . . . involves the disciplined study of what the world is like to people who have learned to see, hear, speak, think and act in ways that are different. Rather than *studying people,* ethnography means *learning from people.* (p. 3)

In the exercise described below, you will learn from people by observing them as they participate in an activity that involves an area of media usage not dealt with elsewhere in this book—playing video games.

## Studying Video Game Players

In this exercise, you will observe a group of video game players. Participant observation generally involves the study of some group of which the researcher is not a part, but it is possible that some students doing this exercise are themselves serious video game players. If you are such a student, try to find some video game players who are somehow different from you (from a different socioeconomic or ethnic or racial group) to observe, to get as much distance as possible. (Some scholars consider it an advantage to investigate a group that one knows about, because this can mean the researcher has some inside information of interest. The problem, however, is maintaining objectivity.) Or you can investigate some alternative media-using group, such as the patrons of coffee shops that have Internet connections or people who attend *Star Trek* conventions.

Here are some of the things you should include in the notes you make while observing the group you have chosen:

1. Indicate where the video game parlor you are studying is located and take note of the significance of the location relative to those who play games in the video game parlor.

2. Record how much time you spend observing. Include how many times you go to the video game parlor and how long you spend there each time.

3. Record the number of male and female video game players and any other demographic information you can: age, ethnicity, race, estimated socioeconomic class, grade in school, style of dress, and so on.

4. Record, as best you can, how much time each person spends playing games, in general, and how long each player plays each game.

5. Describe the style of dress of the various players.

6. Record any ritualistic or highly structured or patterned behavior in the players. Are there cliques? Are certain players "opinion leaders" and others basically submissive? What do the players take for granted?

Get to know some players who will talk with you ("informants"), to help you understand how the group functions and how its members think. You may want to ask questions such as the following:

- What is your favorite game?
- Why do you like it? What's special about it?
- If this wasn't always your favorite game, what was your favorite before you switched?
- Why do you like video games?
- How much time do you spend playing video games here?
- How many times do you go to video game parlors in a typical week?
- Why do you come to this video game parlor rather than go to other ones?
- How much money do you spend in a typical week playing video games? Where do you get the money to play?
- Do you think there's a difference between the games boys play and the games girls play? If so, what is it?
- Is there a difference between the ways boys and girls play? If so, what is it?

While doing your research, be sure to write down any statements that players make that you think might be significant and might help people understand the mind-set of video game players.

See whether you can find any hidden or latent functions (functions that video game players do not recognize) to video game playing. Also, get some information on the development of the video game industry over the years (especially information about how large it is, how much money is spent on video games outside the home, and similar material) and relate your findings to these economic data.

## Writing a Report on Your Participant Observation

1. Begin with an introduction that gives your reader information about the video game parlor you chose, its location, the games it has, brief descriptions of the games, and other general information. If you consulted any articles or books about video game players, indicate what you found.

2. Tell the reader what interesting data you found about the demographic aspects of the video game players. You should make a chart to display your data, so your reader can see easily what you've found.

3. Give your views, based on your observations, on any latent or unintended and unrecognized functions of video game playing for the players involved. The manifest functions of video game playing are amusement and entertainment, but the latent functions may involve all kinds of things that the players do not recognize. Use quotations from the video players when suitable.

4. Discuss any problems you had in doing your participant observation and any difficulties you had in generalizing from your rather limited exercise in this kind of research.

5. Discuss the benefits of participant observation and what you learned from the experience.

6. If you have studied video game players from different ethnic, racial, gender, and socioeconomic classes, describe the differences (if any) you have observed among the various players and discuss what these differences suggest.

Historians do not recapture or reconstruct the past when they analyze history; they interpret it according to surviving evidence and conceptual frameworks. All of past reality can never be known to them because not all evidence remains. Furthermore, historians do not choose to deal even with all the facts derivable from the available evidence. They confine their interests to man's past, but not even all of that concerns them, for they further select from these data those parts that can be organized according to some interpretation or theory. Thus an historical synthesis is a highly selective account of a postulated past reality. Theory, in the most general sense, is crucial to every phase of historiography.

Robert E. Berkhofer, Jr., **A Behavioral Approach to Historical Analysis** (1969, p. 23)

# Chapter 12

## Historical Research: Images of Shopping Malls in the Popular Press

For this chapter you will make a historical study of the evolution of shopping malls in the United States and the ways these malls have been characterized in the popular press (or, as an alternative, you may focus on scholarly journals and books). Shopping malls have played an important role in American commercial culture and society, and you will find it interesting to see how they have evolved over the years and to examine how Americans' attitudes toward them have also changed.

### Problems With a Historical Perspective

History, in the context of this chapter, is understood to be an interpretation of the past made by historians (or writers in any field taking a historical approach). History is not a record of the past, but a selection of data and other information made by historians, as Berkhofer (1969) points out. Historians do the best job they can, using the evidence they have, to make sense of whatever it is they are writing about. But historians differ about what they think is important. Is history the record of kings and great figures, or is it the story of the "people"? Should we concentrate on what various rulers have done, or should we study records of wheat production and trade?

The term *evidence* is particularly apt here. It is useful to think of a historian as being very much like a lawyer, trying to suggest what is important and what is not important from information that is available and building an argument based on that evidence. One problem is that historians (and lawyers) don't always agree about the validity of data and the importance of various events.

You can take any important event in American history and find numerous different interpretations of that event—written by historians with different perspectives or, to use Berkhofer's term, "theories" about history. Historians, then, often argue with one another about the details of many events:

1. What happened?
2. When did it happen?
3. Why did it happen?
4. What does it mean (what significance does it have)?
5. What impact has it had on society and culture?

There are some historians, for example, who believe that American history is, in essence, a record of consensus, whereas there are others who argue that it is, basically, a record of conflict. Consensus historians, as you can imagine, "read" American history quite differently from conflict historians.

In addition, different schools of thought or approaches to history become popular and then fade away, as they are eclipsed by other approaches. There are many kinds of historians, including Marxist historians, psychohistorians (who use psychoanalytic theory to analyze important figures), economic historians, and quantitative historians. History, in short, is an art, not a science.

## Advantages of a Historical Approach

Historical research offers an investigator interesting ways of looking at how our ideas about various topics, events, and personalities have evolved. Such research can be inexpensive to conduct, and many of the materials (at least those you will need for this exercise) are relatively easy to work with. All you will need for purposes of this exercise is a decent library. If you have access to a computer and information on the Internet, that is even better.

Consider, for example, a subject similar to the one you will be undertaking: the image of professional athletes in the popular press. By *popular press,* I mean newspapers, magazines, and popular books (we could add radio and television commentaries also, but collecting data from those sources is more difficult). By researching historical coverage of athletes in the popular press, you can see for yourself how Americans' ideas about athletes have evolved over the years, from (to simplify matters somewhat) adulation to rather negative attitudes in many cases. You might be able to find articles about certain events (such as when Mike Tyson bit the ear of Evander Holyfield) that you think have been of major importance in leading to these changes. You could cite these events and make an argument about their significance. There is something exciting about investigating a subject from a historical perspective and drawing conclusions. In the case of Americans' attitudes toward professional athletes, you may conclude that our attitudes have changed—or, if you wish to be cautious, you may say only that they *seem* to have changed.

## Disadvantages of a Historical Approach

One problem with a historical approach is that you can never be certain how accurate or correct your sources are. When you read articles by sports writers, are you getting factual information, opinion, or some combination of both? How do you separate fact from opinion or interpretation? This is one of the most common problems that historical researchers face. (Sometimes, one discovers that what one thought was a fact is in reality a writer's interpretation or opinion.)

It can also be difficult to find material on the topic of interest; sometimes a researcher has no clear-cut way to determine if particular material even exists. Consider the example of a collision between two automobiles: Often, the witnesses to such an accident will offer wildly differing descriptions of what happened. If this is the case for something as simple as a car crash, imagine how difficult it can be to find the truth concerning more complex events involving human motives, beliefs, conflicts, and so on. If you have statistical data, can you be sure the data are accurate and that all the important and relevant data are available? How do you interpret these data?

## Assignment: A Historical Study of the Images of Shopping Malls

You are to study the *images* that shopping malls have had in the United States over the years. That is, you will investigate the way malls have been written about in the U.S. popular press, which means newspapers and general-circulation magazines. (You can add popular books to this list to enable you to do a more in-depth analysis, but to make things easier, you may want to limit your research to newspapers or to magazines. Let's assume you will use only periodicals.)

You will want to take the following steps in your research:

1. Find the earliest newspaper and general-circulation magazine articles you can on shopping malls. Look at some of the important newspapers, such as the *New York Times, Wall Street Journal,* and *Los Angeles Times,* and at magazines such as *Time* and *Newsweek.* If you have access to the Internet, you should also use it, but not until you've done research in the library. The Internet should serve as an addition to traditional library research, not a substitute for it.
2. Find out when and where the first shopping mall was built in the United States. How was it described in the press of the time? What terms were used?
3. Explore how shopping malls are classified. How have they evolved over the years?
4. Look for analyses and interpretations dealing with the social, economic, and cultural significance and impact of shopping malls.
5. Find articles about malls in contemporary publications and compare them with earlier works to see if there have been any changes in the way malls are written about.

### Writing a Report on Your Historical Research

1. Begin your report with an introduction in which you describe how you went about your research.

2. If you found that there have been significant changes in the images of shopping malls over the years in the American popular press, tell what they are. Be sure to provide quotations from early articles and from more contemporary ones so that your reader can compare them. That is, offer your reader evidence.

3. If you found no changes, show this by providing quotations from the periodicals you investigated. Make certain, to the extent you can, that you are being fair and not neglecting any important articles, either negative or positive. Offer an explanation of why you think there have been no significant changes in the images of malls.

4. Conclude with a discussion of the problems you faced in doing this research and any qualifications you would offer as to your findings.

Basically, all social science is comparative. Social scientists, sociologists included, seek to formulate generalizations which apply to all human behavior; to do this, of course, involves specifying the conditions under which a given relationship among two or more variables holds true. . . .

In attempting to account for a specific pattern of behavior which has occurred in a given part of the world, for example, the causal relationship (if any) between the emergence of Protestantism and the rise of capitalism, it is clearly necessary to engage in comparative research. Without examining social relations in different nations, it is impossible to know to what extent a given factor actually has its suggested effect. For example, if it is true that the German Ständesstaat (rigid status system) has played an important role in determining the authoritarian pattern of German politics, how does it happen that a similar structure in Sweden is associated with a very different political culture? Again, the fact that the American rates of mobility are not uniquely greater than those in countries with class-conscious politics obviously raises a number of questions: Why has there been consensus concerning the relative "openness" of American society?

Seymour Martin Lipset, "Some Methodological Considerations,"
in Seymour Martin Lipset and Richard Hofstadter (Eds.),
**Sociology and History: Methods** (1968, p. 34)

# Chapter 13

Comparative Analysis: Images
of Disneyland (and Disney World)
in the American Popular
and Scholarly Press

Comparative analysis is one of the most common approaches to media research. The quotation from Lipset presented on the opposite page makes an important point—our knowledge tends to be based on our observation of similarities and differences among phenomena. In comparative research, we look for differences; by observing differences, we gain perspective. In the exercise for this chapter, you will investigate the differences between the popular press and the scholarly press in the United States in how Disneyland is viewed and presented. (Note: My use of the name *Disneyland* throughout this chapter should be understood to cover both Disneyland and Disney World. In your analysis you may want to focus on either or both of these parks.)

## Comparative Research

Comparative research, for purposes of this chapter, is research that compares and contrasts how something is done in one place or by one group of people or members of one society with the way the same thing is done in a different place or by a different group of people or society, generally at around the same time. Specifically regarding this chapter's exercise, you will conduct comparative research into the way Disneyland has been written about by writers in the U.S. popular press and by American academics and scholars (whose work is published in scholarly journals, chapters in scholarly books, and the like).

Some of the comparisons that may be made in comparative research are as follows:

- differences over space
- *here* contrasted with *there*
- *us* contrasted with *them*
- *articles in the popular press* compared with *scholarly articles*

### Problems With a Comparative Perspective

When conducting comparative research, investigators must take care not to compare apples and oranges. The subjects of the comparison must be similar in some meaningful way; otherwise any differences found will be irrelevant. We can compare green apples with red apples, or one variety of red apple with a different variety of red apple, but it doesn't make sense to compare an apple and an orange (unless the subject of the research is differences between, say, noncitrus and citrus fruits).

Another potential problem in using a comparative approach is that it requires the subjects of comparison to take place or to exist in the same general time frame. If this is not the case, the analysis is really a historical one, and it will probably be flawed, because the researcher may not realize that he or she is mixing historical interpretation and comparative analysis.

### Advantages of a Comparative Approach

The main advantage of a comparative approach to research is that it offers a way of understanding the groups, institutions, cultures, or societies being studied. As the Swiss linguist Ferdinand de Saussure (1966) explains, "Concepts are purely differential and defined not by their positive content but negatively by their relations with other terms of the system" (p. 117); or, as Saussure adds, the "most precise characteristic" of concepts "is in being what the others are not." Nothing, from Saussure's perspective, has any meaning in itself; everything has meaning only relative to something else.

Let me offer an example of the importance of comparisons. Suppose you discover that the typical family of four in the United States had a total income of $25,000 in 1997. Is that a lot of money? Is that family rich? When you compare that amount of money with the annual income of a typical family in another country, you get some idea what that $25,000 means. You also have to think about the cost of living in different countries. It is also helpful to compare the $25,000 figure with official estimates of the poverty line in the United States. If $25,000 is only a few thousand dollars more than the annual income of people living in poverty, then it doesn't seem like such a good income. It has been said that "comparisons are odious." That may be so, but they can tell us a great deal.

## Disadvantages of a Comparative Approach

When you make a comparative analysis, you face a big problem—that of the reliability of the material you are working with. If you have statistical data, can you be sure the data are accurate and that all the important and relevant data are available? If you are relying on written material, do you know if the writer is biased in some way? What evidence do writers offer for their opinions and judgments?

(There may also be, in certain cases, language problems in comparative analyses. For example, if you are comparing scholarly American and French views of Disneyland, it helps if you can read French, so you can read the French authors' material yourself, rather than being able to study only material that has been translated into English. It is also helpful if you understand French culture, or you might miss particular allusions or subtle points made by the French writers. The French sociologist Jean Baudrillard has, in fact, written about Disneyland in his book *America*, and other French scholars have written on Disneyland as well.)

## A Comparative Research Project

You are to study the image of Disneyland as portrayed in the American popular press compared with in the scholarly press. That is, you will investigate the way Disneyland has been written about in the popular periodical press in the United States (which, for our purposes, means newspapers and general-circulation magazines) and compare what you find in these articles with what you find about Disneyland in scholarly articles and books.

1. Find any newspaper and general-circulation magazine articles you can on Disneyland. Look at some of the important newspapers, such as the *New York Times, Wall Street Journal,* and *Los Angeles Times,* and at magazines such as *Time* and *Newsweek.* You may also want to examine magazines that tend to be somewhat critical of American culture, such as *The Nation.*
2. Find articles and books written by American scholars (such as sociologists, anthropologists, psychologists, and culture critics) that deal with Disneyland.
3. Study the articles on Disneyland that you found in the popular press and note the important points (positive and negative) made in these articles.
4. Study the articles in American academic and scholarly magazines about Disneyland and note the important points made by the authors.

## Writing a Report on Your Comparative Research

1. Begin your report with an introduction in which you describe how you went about your research.

2. Compare how the popular and scholarly articles analyze, describe, and portray Disneyland. Discuss any important similarities and differences.

3. Did your research help you to formulate any ideas about how to explain the incredible popularity of Disneyland with the American public? If so, discuss them.

4. Did your comparative research lead you to any interesting insights about American culture and society? Do you think that Disneyland is (or ever was) "the happiest place on earth"? Explain your answer.

5. Conclude your report with a discussion of the problems you faced in doing your research and any qualifications you would offer about your findings.

# Part II
## Writing and Thinking

Metaphor is pervasive in everyday life, not just in language but in thought and action. Our ordinary conceptual system, in terms of which we both think and act, is fundamentally metaphorical in nature.

The concepts that govern our thought are not just matters of the intellect. They also govern our everyday functioning, down to the most mundane details. Our concepts structure what we perceive, how we get around in the world, and how we relate to other people. Our conceptual system thus plays a central role in defining our everyday realities. If we are right in suggesting that our conceptual system is largely metaphorical, then the way we think, what we experience, and what we do every day is very much a matter of metaphor.

George Lakoff and Mark Johnson,
**Metaphors We Live By** (1980, p. 3)

# Chapter 14
## Writing With Style

Rhetoric, as I have discussed in Chapter 7, is technically defined as the "science of persuasion." For purposes of this chapter, however, we will consider rhetoric as it applies to effective writing. I discuss below a number of techniques that can be used in writing so that readers will find it interesting, entertaining, informative, fascinating, and easy to understand.

It is not a bad idea (even if it isn't true) to assume that all readers are reluctant and would rather be watching television. Thus in order to get people to read something you have written, you must take pains to attract their attention, gain their interest, and make it easy (and desirable) for them to continue reading what you have written. You must cater to certain needs people have, and appeal to their curiosity—about causes and effects, about how particular things differ from other things, and so on.

A number of rhetorical techniques are discussed below. Many of these techniques are signaled in writing by the use of transitions (Table 14.1 shows some of the more important transitions and their functions). For more on transitional elements, see Exhibit 14.1. We will now consider some of the ways you can make your writing more interesting and appealing.

### Contrast and Comparison

Contrast and comparison are important because, as I have noted elsewhere in this book, we find meaning in things by comparing them (and contrasting them) with other things. *Rich* doesn't mean anything unless there is *poor; intelligent* doesn't mean anything unless there is

**TABLE 14.1**  Rhetorical Transitions and Their Functions

| Offering Examples | Conclusions Reached | Argument Continues |
|---|---|---|
| for example | therefore | furthermore |
| for instance | thus | in addition |
| as an illustration | we find, then | to continue |
| to show this | to sum up | similarly |
| *Contrasting Ideas* | *Causes* | *Effects* |
| but | because | as a result |
| however | since | therefore |
| on the other hand | this leads to | accordingly |
| in contrast | seeing that | as a consequence |
| *Sequence* | *Time Relation* | *Meaning* |
| first | before | this means |
| next | after | we find, then |
| furthermore | meanwhile | this suggests |
| to begin with | at the same time | this tells us |

SOURCE: Adapted from Berger (1990).

*dumb.* Meaning stems from the differentiations we make, and the most significant differentiations involve oppositions. We know that there are rich people, middle-class people, and poor people (and many gradations in between as well), but we commonly think of opposites when making comparisons.

Items or concepts that are contrasted and compared should have something in common; they should fall into the same general category. In writing, we often indicate that we are contrasting concepts through the use of such transitions as "on the other hand" and "in contrast." When we make comparisons, we often use such transitions as "in the same manner" and "by the same token."

## Definitions

Definitions are statements that specify how people use words. That is, a definition tells how people use (or used) a term, the conventions common in using the term, and/or what people "mean" when they

**Exhibit 14.1**

*Transitional Elements*

Here is an example of writing in which transitional elements are used; all bold type has been added to emphasize the transitions. I have selected this passage because it shows how transitions order thinking and because it contains advice of considerable importance and usefulness for writers.

*How Judgments Stop Thought*

A judgment ("He is a fine boy," "It was a beautiful service," "Baseball is a healthful sport," "She is an awful bore") is a conclusion, summing up a large number of previously observed facts. The reader is probably familiar with the fact that students almost always have difficulty in writing themes of the required length because their ideas give out after a paragraph or two. **The reason for this is that** those early paragraphs contain so many judgments that there is little left to be said. When the conclusions are carefully excluded, **however**, and observed facts are given instead, there is never any trouble about the length of papers; **in fact**, they tend to become too long, **since** inexperienced writers, when told to give facts, often give far more than is necessary, **because** they lack discrimination between the important and the trivial.

**Still another** consequence of judgments early in the course of a written exercise—and this applies also to hasty judgments in everyday thought—is the temporary blindness they induce. When, **for example,** a description starts with the words, "He was a real Madison Avenue executive" or "She was a typical hippie," if we continue writing at all, we must make all our later statements consistent with those judgments. **The result is** that all the individual characteristics of this particular "executive" or this particular "hippie" are lost sight of; **and** the rest of the account is likely to deal not with observed facts but with stereotypes and the writer's particular notion (based on previously read stories, movies, pictures, and so forth) of what "Madison Avenue executives" or "typical hippies" are like. The premature judgment, **that is**, often prevents us from seeing what is directly in front of us, **so that** clichés take the place of fresh description. **Therefore**, even if the writer feels sure at the beginning of a written account that the man he is describing is a "real leatherneck" or that the scene he is describing is a "beautiful residential suburb," he will conscientiously keep such notions out of his head, lest his vision be obstructed. He is specifically warned against describing anybody as a "beatnik"—a term (originally applied to literary and artistic Bohemians) which was blown up by sensational journalism and movies into an almost completely fictional and misleading stereotype. If a writer applies the term to any actual living human being, he will have to expend so much energy thereafter explaining what he does *not* mean by it that he will save himself trouble by not bringing it up at all. The same warning applies to "hippies" and other social classifications that tend to submerge the individual in a category.

SOURCE: Hayakawa (1978, p. 40).

use the term. Thus a dictionary is a record that shows how people use words; some dictionaries also show the roots (in Latin, Greek, and other languages) of words.

It is often the case that researchers define words or concepts in certain ways for the purposes of their work. *Violence* is a good example. The amount of violence a researcher finds on television is affected by the way he or she defines the term. Researchers who use a very narrow definition will, logically, find less violence on television than will those who use a very broad, all-encompassing definition (and include, for instance, humorous violence and accidental violence). Because the concept of violence encompasses so many different aspects, researchers in this field must explain how they define television violence and offer reasonable explanations for their definition.

In some cases, it is useful to cite an expert or authority when offering a definition. For example, it has been estimated that anthropologists have offered more than 100 different definitions of *culture*— and countless other definitions have been put forward by literary scholars and other kinds of academics. If you are dealing with culture from an anthropological perspective (and we are doing that in this book), it is a good idea to explain what you mean when you use the word *culture*. The following definition is from Henry Pratt Fairchild's *Dictionary of Sociology and Related Sciences* (1967):

> A collective name for all behavior patterns socially acquired and transmitted by means of symbols; hence a name for all the distinctive achievements of human groups, including not only such items as language, tool-making, industry, art, science, law, government, morals and religion, but also the material instruments or artifacts in which cultural achievements are embodied and by which intellectual cultural features are given practical effect, such as buildings, tools, machines, communications devices, art objects, etc. (p. 80)

According to this definition, everybody has culture; indeed, to be human is to become, in the anthropological sense of the term, cultured. This definition gives us a considerably different perspective on things from one that equates culture with the "elite" arts, such as opera, classical music, ballet, serious novels, and poetry.

It is generally a good idea to define terms that may be unfamiliar to your readers or that you are using in a special way.

## Cause and Effect

Cause and effect form probably the most common kind of "explanation" we use. When we explain something, we usually try to describe what brought the situation about. What "caused" the Civil War? What are the "causes" of poverty?

One of the reasons we are interested in causes is that we believe we can gain some measure of control over things once we have determined what causes them. If you have an upset stomach, it is helpful to know what caused it, so you can take the right kind of medicine and so you can avoid eating foods in the future that you know you have trouble digesting. Or maybe it wasn't the kind of food you ate but where you ate it. Perhaps you had dinner in a restaurant that wasn't as clean as it should be?

Thus we search for causes to help us understand and explain effects, so we can prevent effects we don't want and generate effects we do want. The basic dimension we deal with is time. The cause, naturally, comes before the effect—but just because Y occurred after X doesn't mean Y was caused by X. Assuming that something is a cause because it precedes an effect is known as the *post hoc, ergo propter hoc* (after, therefore as a result of) fallacy. Consider, for example, an upset stomach. There can be any number of reasons a person might have an upset stomach: food poisoning, too much food, too much exercise after eating, food allergies, and so on. When discussing cause and effect, then, it is generally a good idea to qualify your statements. You might say that there is reason to believe that something causes a given effect, or that something seems to cause or might be causing the effect.

## Classification

The purpose of classification is to make clear relationships that may not be immediately evident. Classification involves taking some collection or group of people or objects or events that have something in common and showing what they share. That is, we take a group related by some common attribute or attributes and break the group down further into mutually exclusive subgroups—depending upon what we want to find out.

For example, take a group of students in one of your classes. What they have in common that makes them a "class" is that they are in the same room with the same teacher taking the same course at the same time. This group can be broken down into smaller groups in terms of such characteristics as socioeconomic class, race, religion, gender, major, hair color, and marital status. By classifying the individuals who make up groups we often find interesting information. Some subgroups may be underrepresented, others overrepresented. You may discover that class members are similar in a number of different ways, and that may be important. There are any number of ways of classifying the members of any group, depending upon the purpose to be served.

Sometimes, instead of breaking a group of persons or things into subclasses that are related in some way, it is useful to do the opposite, setting up a classification system for some grouping of seemingly disparate people or events. In this case, the task is to find relationships among them and set up a classification scheme that shows how they are related.

Marketing researchers are always coming up with new classification schemes that divide the American public into various groupings. One example is the VALS (Values and Life Styles) typology created by SRI International, which includes three main categories: the need-driven, the outer-directed, and the inner-directed. There are a number of subcategories under each of these main categories:

| need-driven | outer-directed | inner-directed |
|---|---|---|
| survivors | belongers | I-am-me |
| sustainers | emulators | experiential |
| achievers | societally conscious | |

The idea behind VALS is that if marketers understand what the people in each of these groupings and subgroupings are like, they can direct advertising to them in a more intelligent and effective manner. Different appeals would be used to sell products to emulators (who imitate others) than to achievers (who tend to be individualists), for instance.

## Analysis

Analysis is similar to classification, except that instead of being concerned with a collection of items, analysis—as I am using the term—is concerned with one item or entity. Classification involves breaking a group down into subgroups and showing how they are related. Analysis, in contrast, involves separating something into its component parts or elements in order to make the relationships clearer and to gain information.

Consider, for example, the drug crisis stemming from crack cocaine. An analysis of this crisis might consider such matters as the production of crack; the distribution of crack; various kinds of other drugs available; the reasons some people use crack and others don't; the impact of crack on individuals, families (especially babies born suffering crack addition), and society; ways of preventing crack use and other drug abuse; and new drugs that might compete with or displace crack (such as "ice"). We analyze something such as the crack crisis to see what the component parts are and to get a better sense of how to deal with it. Our analysis may suggest that a certain course of action is most likely to help us achieve the results we want. We analyze, then, to understand.

## Examples

The use of examples is one of the best ways to make your writing clear. Explanations alone tend to be rather abstract, because they generally have to cover a wide variety of possibilities. When you move down the ladder of abstraction from explanation to examples, however, you provide a means for your reader to see more clearly what you are talking about.

Providing examples is like providing a kind of evidence to help document a generalization. An example is a "case history" that is both specific and has implications beyond itself. In using examples, of course, you must be sure that they are relevant to the point you are making.

In writing, there are a number of transitional devices you can use to help cue your reader that an example is to follow. Phrases such as "for example" and "to illustrate" let your reader know that you are going to offer specifics.

For example, the general concept of "juvenile delinquency" is rather abstract, but you can show your reader what you mean by describing specific cases of young people who have broken windows in a school, set fires, stolen cars, held up gas stations, mugged old ladies, and so on. It is always a good idea to *show* people what you are talking about, and you can do this by using examples. It is also useful to move back and forth between generalizations or abstractions and examples. If you write at too high a level of abstraction, your writing lacks interest; if you deal only in examples, you can't make any interesting generalizations.

## Description and Detail

Description is another important element of a writing style that provides readers with material they will find interesting and illuminating. Many people do not have what might be described as a "developed" style of writing. Their prose has no flesh attached to the bare bones of their ideas; their writing lacks detail.

To see the difference that description and detail make, think of a meal as it might be described by two different people. The first person writes, "We had a delicious meal at Pierre's last night." This is undeveloped writing; it offers little information, telling you something but providing nothing to support the general adjective *delicious*. The second writer, a restaurant critic, describes in great detail each and every dish, how it was made, how it was served, what it tasted like, what it looked like, and so on. The second writer might have written:

> We began with a dish of escargot—six plump escargot, swimming in a smooth and exquisitely subtle sauce of butter, garlic, and parsley. The escargot were served on a piping hot china dish. . . .

The description of the meal might take pages, with whole paragraphs devoted to particular dishes, sauces, tastes, and related matters.

When a student complains that he or she doesn't have enough material to write a paper of 5 or 10 pages, it is generally because the student doesn't write in a developed style; that is, he or she has not learned to include enough description and detail. The other side of the matter, of course, is that you must not use description and detail in an inappropriate manner—that is, simply to pad your papers. You have to use some judgment in deciding how much description and detail to include, how and when to offer examples, and how to use any of the other rhetorical techniques discussed above.

## Process

Process is how something works, how something is to be done, what must be done to accomplish something. This might be something as simple as baking a cake or as complicated as carrying out a research project. In writing about process—for example, about how you have conducted a research project, or about how something you have studied works—you need to focus on the steps you have taken or observed. Your descriptions of processes should make clear the activities that made up those processes.

In writing up your findings, it is important that you describe the process through which you conducted your research. This will enable those who read your write-up to follow the way you worked and see whether or not you made any mistakes. Writing about process should be sequential—describe the various steps you took, one after another, in carrying out your research. This includes everything from the assignment of the research method to the writing up of the conclusions.

## Tone

By *tone* in writing, I mean its degree of formality. You determine the proper tone to adopt by considering your audience. If you are writing a letter to a friend, your tone will be much more informal, casual, and conversational than it would be if you were writing a letter to apply for a job or if you were writing a paper for a course.

You should always take the matter of formality or informality into consideration and adopt the appropriate tone. Generally speaking, papers written for courses in schools and universities should be formal in style, unless you have been given instructions to the contrary. You should avoid a casual, conversational tone in research papers, but this does not mean your writing has to be stilted or affected.

In the past, a formal scholarly writer was expected to refer to him- or herself in writing only in the third person ("the author," "this writer," "the researcher") or in the first person plural ("we found," "our research"). Neither of these styles is required any longer in most kinds of writing (although journalists are still discouraged from referring to themselves in the first person).

The main thing about formal writing is not so much the tone, however, as the need to support contentions with evidence and to avoid errors in grammar and in logic. Adopting an elevated or stilted style and using jargon are not substitutes for good thinking and good writing.

## Structure

*Structure* here refers to the organization of a paper—the relationships established among the various parts. In scholarly writing, it is a good idea to make the organization of a paper evident, to describe its structure:

1. Tell the reader, in an introduction, what your thesis is (in a thesis statement).
2. Tell the reader how you will provide convincing evidence to support your thesis.
3. Tell the reader what you did in your research—your results and conclusions, the problems you faced, how you solved them, and so on.

Writing papers is much like teaching. As the formula for teaching is often stated: Tell them what you're going to tell them, tell them, and tell them what you've told them.

It is helpful to provide charts and tables (infographics) to show relationships in a clear and obvious manner. Charts and tables take advantage of the human ability to process visual material in a fast and efficient manner. Let me offer an example. In an essay on *Star Trek*, it was suggested that the Freudian concepts of the id, the ego, and the superego can be applied, respectively, to McCoy, Spock, and Kirk. The id is generally identified with impulses and desires, the ego with rationality and reality testing, and the superego with conscience.

In the above paragraph, all of the distinctions mentioned are buried in the linearity of the written language. The same material can be presented in a simple chart in which all the relationships are immediately evident:

### Psychological Profile of *Star Trek* Characters

| *id* | *ego* | *superego* |
|------|-------|------------|
| impulse | reason | conscience |
| McCoy | Spock | Kirk |

Charts and graphs should be complemented by writing that discusses and expands upon what they show.

Let me suggest a method for making an outline, so your papers will be logically organized and coherent. There are outlining programs for computers, but you can also make good outlines using paper and ink.

1. Take a sheet of blank paper and cut it into 16ths. You can do this easily by folding it over and cutting it into halves, cutting the halves into quarters, and so on. You should do this with two sheets of paper, which means you will end up with 32 small pieces of paper.

2. On each piece of paper write *one concept* that you will discuss in the paper. For example, on one piece you might write your thesis. On another piece, you write one bit of evidence that supports your thesis, and on another you write another bit of evidence. You should continue brainstorming—writing ideas, concepts, examples, what you will—one to a piece of paper, for as long as you can. If you need more pieces of paper, cut more up.

3. Organize the pieces of paper in a coherent and logical manner. Some writers pin the pieces on bulletin boards, others stack them and staple them together. The main thing is that by limiting yourself to one idea, fact, concept, or example per piece of paper, you can change the order of the matters to be discussed in your paper very easily.

4. You should have some kind of an introduction section to your paper, in which you give some kind of background and sense of context and do what you can to interest your readers and stimulate their sense of

curiosity. You should also state your thesis—what you hope to show—in your introduction.

5. In the body of your paper you should offer evidence to support your thesis.

6. In the conclusion of your paper you should explain what you have done and give your interpretations of what you have found. You should also state any qualifications you have to offer, discuss any difficulties you encountered in carrying out your research, and mention any other related considerations.

Remember that the way you write—your voice, your style—plays an important role in how your paper is received. It is always a good idea to write a first draft of a paper, set it aside for a few days, and then revise and rewrite when you can come to it with a fresh mind. Good writing *always* involves revising and rewriting. First drafts can always be improved, and they often contain a number of stylistic and grammatical mistakes. You should write with a sense of obligation to your readers—you must make your writing as interesting and easy to read as possible.

If the reader is lost, it is generally because the writer has not been careful enough to keep him on the path.

This carelessness can take any number of forms. Perhaps a sentence is so excessively cluttered that the reader, hacking his way through the verbiage, simply doesn't know what it means. Perhaps a sentence has been so shoddily constructed that the reader could read it in any of several ways. Perhaps the writer has switched pronouns in mid-sentence, or has switched tenses, so the reader loses track of who is talking or when the action took place. Perhaps Sentence B is not a logical sequence to Sentence A—the writer, in whose head the connection is clear, has not bothered to provide the missing link. Perhaps the writer has used an important word incorrectly by not taking the trouble to look it up. . . .

Faced with these obstacles, the reader is at first a remarkably tenacious bird. He blames himself—he obviously missed something, and he goes back over the mystifying sentence, or over the whole paragraph, piecing it out like an ancient rune, making guesses and moving on. But he won't do this for long. The writer is making him work too hard, and the reader will look for one who is better at his craft.

William Zinsser,
**On Writing Well** (1976, pp. 9, 12)

# Chapter 15

## Avoiding Common Writing Errors

### A Note on Communication

When you come to write up what you have discovered in your research projects, you should remember that your main goal is to convey information to your readers in as clear a manner as possible. There are rules that we must obey when we write, just as there are rules we have to obey when we drive. You have to learn the highway code (and pass a test showing that you know the rules) to drive, and you must obey the rules if you don't want to be in a crash. We can get from point A to point B only because we all know the rules and follow them (more or less).

In the same manner, you have to learn the rules of grammar and follow them if you want others to be able to understand you. You can think of punctuation, for example, as being similar (in function) to stop signs, stop lights, direction signals, and so on. If you run a red light, for example, you could get a ticket, become involved in an accident, or both. And if you don't put a period at the end of a sentence, or don't use commas to indicate where readers are to pause, they will become confused.

What you will be doing, for the most part, is telling your readers the results of your research projects and how you carried them out. This kind of writing, known as expository writing, need not be dull or bland, but it doesn't generally make use of the kind of language used in novels, for example, to entertain readers.

In this chapter I will discuss some of the more common writing mistakes that people tend to make. If you can learn to avoid some of these errors, your writing will be considerably improved. It is, of course, impossible to offer an extensive lesson on grammar in this short chapter; you should have a good grammar book to use as a reference, should you have any problems that are not covered here. In this discussion I will avoid, to the extent it is possible, many of the technical terms commonly used in grammar texts.

## Incomplete Sentences (Sentence Fragments)

A number of years ago a Swiss linguist, Ferdinand de Saussure, suggested that meaning is based on differences. The most important aspect of concepts, he said, is in being what others (concepts) are not. What this tells us is that meaning is tied to relationships. Some kind of a relationship between elements in a sentence has to be created for us to find meaning.

If you complete relationships in your sentences (generally involving a subject, an object, and a verb), they will likely not be incomplete. The secret is to have two elements (at least)—two people, places, things—and a verb to explain the relationship. Let's consider John, Mary, Rover, and philosophy.

> MARY, who has just returned from a trip around the world, during which she explored the Nile, participated in an archaeological dig in India, and climbed Mount Everest, IS MAJORING IN the subject she finds more interesting than any other (though it won't get her a job)—PHILOSOPHY.

All the basic elements in this complicated sentence appear in capital letters, and they form a complete thought: Mary is majoring in philosophy.

Suppose one were to write:

> Because Mary is majoring in philosophy.

This is an incomplete sentence; the word *because* implies that some kind of description of an act or a situation is to follow.

Suppose one were to write:

> Because Mary is majoring in philosophy, she will probably find it hard to get a job.

In this sentence, "Because Mary is majoring in philosophy" is tied to "she," which functions as the subject of the sentence and tells us why Mary probably will have trouble finding a job.

## Fused Sentences

Fused or run-on sentences contain several complete sentences that are not adequately separated. Meaning is based on relationships within sentences and among sentences, so it is important that you don't forget to establish this meaning by using transitions, and that you don't confuse readers with faulty punctuation. We expect to pause, momentarily, between sentences, and if you tie two sentences together without the right punctuation, the reader can get mixed up.

Here is an example of a fused or run-on sentence:

Mary loves philosophy she might find it hard to get a job.

The problem here is that we have two complete sentences—"Mary loves philosophy" and "She might find it hard to get a job"—that are tied together. This problem can be dealt with in several ways. A coordinating conjunction or a phrase could be added to link the two sentences:

Mary loves philosophy, *so* she might find it hard to get a job.

A semicolon could be used to separate the two sentences:

Mary loves philosophy; she might find it hard to get a job.

Note that you would probably not want to use *and* here to join the two sentences because we are dealing, in essence, with cause and effect. *And* would link the two sentences together, but would not show how they are related.

## Faulty Pronoun Reference

A pronoun is a word used in place of a noun or another pronoun that precedes it. We use pronouns because it would be terribly boring to use a person's name (or any noun) over and over again. There are two important rules to remember when you use pronouns:

1. A pronoun refers to a noun or pronoun that comes before it (the antecedent). You must make certain that the relationship between the pronoun and its antecedent is unambiguous.
2. A pronoun must agree with its antecedent in number (singular or plural) and person.

Following are some examples of poor pronoun usage.

Clutching the fried chicken, John got into his car and started eating it.

As this sentence reads now, John appears to be eating his car. We can solve this problem by writing:

John got into his car and started eating some fried chicken.

Here is another mistaken use of pronouns:

Everyone should put their coats away.

In this sentence, the pronoun doesn't agree with its subject. *Everyone* (like a number of other words that seem to be plural) is a singular pronoun and requires a singular verb. We should write:

Everyone should put his or her coat away.

A complete rewrite provides an alternative solution:

Please put your coats away.

## Comma Faults

A comma fault occurs when two sentences are separated by a comma instead of a stronger form of punctuation (a semicolon, a colon, a dash, or a period, depending upon the situation) or a conjunction. A comma signifies a relatively slight pause between elements in a sentence. It cannot separate two sentences, however.

Consider the following sentence:

> Mary and John love each other, she got a job so they could get married.

The comma is not adequate in this situation. One of the following alternatives would be acceptable:

> Mary and John love each other. She got a job so they could get married.

> Mary and John love each other, so she got a job so they could get married.

> Because Mary and John love each other and wish to get married, she got a job.

The problem with the first alternative is that no relationships are made evident, so we have two discrete little sentences. We know that Mary and John love each other *and* that Mary got a job. We can figure things out, but it is better if the relationship is made more evident by a transition or some other device.

## Faulty Verb Agreement

Verbs must agree in number with their subjects. This is necessary to make relationships evident. If a sentence has a plural subject and a singular verb, we become confused. Let us return to John, Mary, and Rover. Let's assume that John loves Rover, Mary loves Rover, and Rover loves both John and Mary.

If we see the word *loves,* we know we are dealing with a single subject:

John loves Rover.

Mary loves Rover.

But if we are dealing with John and Mary together (the equivalent of *they*) we must use the plural verb *love.*

John and Mary love Rover.

If we are focusing on Rover (the equivalent of *he*), we use the singular verb form:

Rover loves John and Mary.

The verb *love* is conjugated as follows:

- *singular:* I love; you love; he/she/it loves
- *plural:* we love; you (plural) love; they love


## Spelling and Erratic Syllabication

A word is either spelled correctly or spelled incorrectly. The only way to be sure that a word is spelled the way you think it is spelled is to check a dictionary. If you write with a word processor, there is a good chance your program has a spell checker built into it. You should use the spell checker after you have finished the first draft of your write-up. If you don't have a spell checker or don't use word processing, use a regular dictionary to check any word that you are not certain about.

At the ends of typed lines, words can be broken only in certain places, at syllable endings. The only way to be sure about a word's correct syllable breaks is to refer to a dictionary. In general, a good rule is to avoid any end-of-line word breaks in your papers—that way you can be sure you won't make a mistake in syllabication.

## Common Errors Based on Confusions

The material that follows is adapted from my chapter on writing errors in *Scripts: Writing for Radio and Television* (1990):

*Two/too/to.* People often become confused when using these words. Here are the correct ways to use them:

*Too* refers to degree. "Too many, too few, too soon, too late."
*Two* is a number. "I want two scripts. I need two actors."
*To* is a preposition. "I am going to Paris, then to London."

*You're/your.* Correct uses of these forms are as follows:

*Your* denotes possession. "I like your dress."
*You're* is a contraction. It ties together *you* and *are*. "That's right, you're correct."

*There/their/they're.* These confuse many people also.

*There* stands for a place. "I'm going there in June."
*Their* denotes possession. "Someone stole their suitcases."
*They're* is a contraction. It ties together *they* and *are*. "They're a wonderful couple."

*Its/it's.* Correct use of these is important, too.

*Its* involves possession. "The fox returned to its lair."
*It's* is a contraction. It ties together *it* and *is*. "It's my birthday."

*Who's/whose.* Correct use of these avoids confusion.

*Whose* involves possession. "Whose book is this?"
*Who's* is a contraction. It ties together *who* and *is*. "Who's coming to your party?"

### Padded, Wordy Writing

Writers who are padding use 25 words to say what can be said in 5 words, or repeat themselves and say the same things in different ways. Students writing term papers often pad because they don't have enough ideas and are required to write a certain number of words; they write in a verbose manner and repeat themselves.

> *padded:* I would like to state that I believe . . .
> *better:* I think . . .

### Incoherent Writing

Incoherent writing is writing that doesn't flow, that jumps around and leaves the reader or listener confused. One way to write coherently is to use transitions to guide the reader along. Transitions tell the reader what to expect. If, for example, you write "on the one hand" about something, a reader can expect to find "on the other hand" as well—that is, information on the other side of the subject.

Incoherence also is found in primer-style writing. "Look, John. There is Spot. See Spot run. See Spot chase the ball." Primer-style material is constructed of very short, very simple sentences—the kind we find in books written for very young children. This kind of writing is generally inappropriate in works for adults.

### Unclear Writing

Unclear writing is writing that is hard to understand; it is confusing and ambiguous at best, and sometimes it is unintelligible. Such writing usually contains many grammatical errors and improper use of language. Sometimes unclear writing is substandard and does not follow the rules and conventions of English grammar. Such things as run-on sentences, misplaced modifiers, faulty pronoun references, and shifts in person and number can make writing unclear. Sometimes unclear writing has so many things wrong with it that it is hard to know where to start to try to correct it.

Writers should always strive to produce prose that is clear and intelligible. What happens in some cases is that writers forget to include material they have stored in their heads that might make their writing clear. They know what they mean to write, but what they put down confuses the reader, who does not have access to this hidden information. Other individuals simply lack the needed knowledge of grammar and language use to produce intelligible writing.

## Awkward Writing

Awkward writing is writing that is stiff or otherwise ungainly. Usually this is because the sentence construction and language use are poor. The awkward writer lacks grace, is clumsy—like a dancer who knows the steps for a dance but doesn't execute them very well.

In some cases, awkward writing results from an author's inadvertent repetition of sentence structure ("I believe" followed by "I think" followed by "I want to say," and so on). Such repetition often shows up when a writer has learned only one way to construct a sentence (e.g., subject, verb, object) and so repeats this structure over and over again.

Reading your papers out loud is a good way to find awkward passages. If you find some of your writing to be severely flawed, often the best way to deal with it is to replace it with new material, rather than try to fix up old problems. Rewriting instead of revising can often save you a good deal of time and effort.

## Trite Expressions and Clichés

"Last, but not least," let me end this chapter with a brief discussion of trite expressions and clichés—you should avoid these, as they say, "like the plague." Trite expressions and clichés, like the ones I've just used, are shopworn phrases that people sometimes use because they are convenient and understandable. Unfortunately, they are also boring and overused, and you should find other ways of expressing yourself when possible. Sometimes, of course, a cliché expresses an idea perfectly and is useful, but most of the time you should try to avoid such writing crutches.

**Final Thoughts**

In this chapter I have dealt with some of the most common errors people make when they write and problems often found in writing. Because of space constraints, I can alert you here only to some of the worst offenders. Every writer should have a good dictionary, a thesaurus, and a grammar book, and should make constant use of them. We all forget, from time to time, the various rules of grammar or how to spell some words. That's natural. But when we write, we have an obligation to our audience to write correctly; it's the least we can do.

If you use a word processor, I suggest that after you have used the spell checker you print out your first draft and make your revisions on the hard copy. In my experience, making revisions at the keyboard, on the screen, just doesn't work very well. And if you revise your papers four or five times, which many writers tell us is necessary, you'll avoid a good deal of eyestrain, too. Remember, also, to double-space all material.

The ability to recognize faulty arguments and to understand why they are faulty is a difficult skill to develop, yet it is an important skill. Faulty arguments are often hard to recognize because they are both appealing and deceptive. They are particularly important objects of study because they attempt to persuade an audience to alter ideas, values, beliefs, attitudes, or actions on the basis of misleading premises or faulty reasoning. Precisely because the purpose of argument is to persuade audiences to accept sound, well-supported claims, we should avoid practices that lead them to base decisions on erroneous inferences and assumptions.

Barbara Warnick and Edward S. Inch, **Critical Thinking and Communication: The Use of Reason in Argument** (1989, p. 127)

# Chapter 16

## Avoiding Common Reasoning Errors

### Writing and Thinking

The purpose of this chapter is to focus attention on some of the common errors people often make in reasoning—errors that make their conclusions questionable. If someone reading one of your papers finds mistakes in your chain of thinking, he or she will have good reason to suspect that your conclusions are not correct. My concern here is not with formal logic, but with "commonsense" aspects of thinking and reasoning errors that you may make because you are careless or confused.

Writing and thinking are intimately connected. You can be a wonderful literary stylist, but if your thinking is full of holes nobody will take what you write about your research seriously. You may be a great talker, but it is only when you commit your ideas to paper and show what you have done (and offer evidence so that others can evaluate your ideas) that we can see whether or not your research is of any value and whether or not you make sense. In the same vein, of course, you can conduct wonderful research and be full of marvelous ideas, but if you can't express yourself correctly (using proper grammar), readers of your reports will be skeptical when they are not confused. What follows is a discussion of a number of common errors people inadvertently (usually) make in their thinking.

### Stacking the Deck

*Stacking the deck* refers to the use of only selected instances in making an argument. For example, you use only material that supports your conclusions and pay no attention to information that contradicts those conclusions. (The allusion here is to playing cards. You arrange the deck so the cards are distributed the way you want them to be, and not the way they would be distributed if the deck had not been tampered with.) When you use selected instances, you may be telling the truth, but you are not telling the whole truth, and by avoiding certain information you end up with a distorted and incorrect picture of whatever it is you are describing.

Stacking the deck is not always done on purpose. When Franklin Delano Roosevelt was running for the presidency against Alf Landon in 1936, a magazine, the *Literary Digest*, took a postcard poll, and on the basis of the poll announced that Landon would defeat Roosevelt. The error the magazine made was in obtaining its list of people to be polled from telephone directories, a decision that eliminated from the sample large numbers of poor people who did not have phones (phones were much more expensive then, relatively speaking, and only the wealthier elements in society could afford them). Roosevelt received 26.7 million votes to Landon's 16.6 million votes in the election. Landon carried only Maine and Vermont, which led to the political wisecrack, often used in discussions of presidential elections, "As Maine goes, so goes Vermont."

Inadvertently, then, the *Literary Digest* stacked the deck by polling only people who would be most likely to vote for Republicans. You must be careful in making your arguments that you do not unintentionally stack the deck.

## Appealing to Authority

Appealing to authority as proof that certain ideas are correct is generally dangerous. On the other hand, in many cases there is no other way to support your arguments; you can't avoid *some* use of authorities. The world is now so complex that none of us can master all fields and subfields, so we tend, naturally, to look for experts and those who (we hope) speak impartially and on the basis of authority.

There are certain problems involved with using the work of authorities to prove your points. For instance, have you chosen a person who is an authority in the area under discussion or in a different field? A doctor may be an authority in some area of medicine but may know little about finance or politics. When you cite authorities, you must use people who are authorities in the appropriate fields of expertise, or your citations will be spurious.

And what do you do when experts disagree? This is frequently the case. Authorities have different perspectives on some subjects, cite different kinds of evidence, and come to different conclusions. In such situations you can only try to figure out which authorities seem to have the best evidence and support for their contentions. We often find this kind of dilemma when we listen to hearings held before some congressional committee. Experts with widely differing points of view testify, and it is difficult to determine who is right. Sometimes, one expert is right about one matter and a different expert is right about another.

The moral of this disquisition is that you must be very careful when you cite authorities. Just because a person is famous or has excellent credentials does not mean that he or she is correct on all matters (or doesn't have some ideological or political notions that color his or her view). If you are going to rely on the works of authorities, as in the case of library research, try to cite the most recent research available from books and journals that are scholarly, and not partisan or ideological.

## Emotionalism

There is a famous joke about a minister who scribbled notes in the margin of his sermon—"Argument weak here . . . shout!" The use of emotionally loaded words is often a way of trying to conceal a lack of logic. If you can get people excited, they won't exercise much discretion and won't be too concerned with whether or not you are telling the truth. We find this technique used a great deal in advertising, which often attempts to motivate people to buy certain products or services on nonrational grounds.

Some of the techniques that might be used to appeal to people's emotions include the following:

1. *Appealing to people's general prejudices:* The speaker or writer uses slogans and insulting terms ("better dead than Red"; eggheads) to stir people up.
2. *Discrediting the person making an argument:* The speaker or writer shifts attention away from an argument to the person making the argument

and attacks him or her on personal grounds. This is known as an *ad hominem* (against the man) argument.

3. *Associating one's point of view with famous individuals:* The speaker or writer tries to use the prestige of some famous individual (George Washington, Abraham Lincoln, Ronald Reagan, Albert Einstein) to convince people of the correctness of his or her point of view. He or she attempts to "transfer" belief in the famous person to belief in an argument (this is an example of what is sometimes called a "halo effect").

4. *Bluffing:* The speaker or writer uses an extremely confident tone to hide a weak argument. Bluffers seem so certain that they are right and argue with such a sense of security that we sometimes get carried along and don't examine their arguments as carefully as we should. Bluffing can be done orally or by adopting a writing style that is supremely self-confident in nature.

## Overgeneralizing

The word *generalization* comes from the Latin word *genus* (kind, class) and refers to a statement that is applicable to every member of some class or group. The critical concept here is *every.* When you make a generalization about a group, unless you qualify it in some manner, your statement must cover every member of that group. One contrary instance negates your generalization. Therefore, it is a good rule to avoid using words such as *all* or *every,* unless you are certain that they are correct and that no contrary instances will be found.

Researchers tend to use language that qualifies their generalizations, phrases such as "as a rule" or "tends to be the case" or "generally are." These phrases slightly weaken the generalization and take into account the possibility of contrary instances.

Does this mean we should never use generalizations? Not at all. Generalizations often convey valuable information. A generalization states that certain relationships tend to be constant. We need this information to function in society. If all we do is relate case studies and are too specific, people don't learn anything from what we write. We need to be able to generalize, but we must be careful not to overgeneralize. That is, we should not generalize from too limited a number of cases studied or examples and we should not make generalizations that are too strong (using *all* or *every*).

## Statements in Which <u>Some</u> Is True, But <u>All</u> Is Implied

A friend of mine (during my Army days) was a confirmed Anglophile. He wore tweed jackets, smoked expensive English tobacco in his English pipe, read English literature, and dreamed about English girls. By chance, he had an opportunity to spend a couple of weeks in England, and he came back a changed man. He had thought that everyone in England would be like the English people he saw on television or heard on the radio—cultivated, aristocratic diplomats and actors who spoke what is called "the received pronunciation" and symbolized England for him. What he found, upon visiting England, was that he had held unrealistic stereotypes of the English. There are, of course, a considerable number of English people who speak beautifully, who are cultured and cultivated, and who lived up to my friend's expectations. But England (and Great Britain as a whole) is also full of working-class people who speak in a variety of accents (some almost unintelligible to American ears).

My friend had assumed that what was true of some people from England (the diplomats and others he saw on television) was true of all the people in England. On the basis of a very limited and unrealistic sampling of English men and women, he made unrealistic generalizations about what all the English are like. In a like manner, we often fall into the trap of making statements that may be true of some but are most definitely *not* true of all. Often these statements include the word *the*—as in "the English" or "the Jews" or "the Catholics" or "the Blacks"—or *they* (standing for entire groups of one kind or another). Our minds tend to work by trying to make generalizations on the basis of whatever information we have on hand. All too often, however, we make faulty generalizations and overgeneralize. We call these overgeneralizations *stereotypes* when they deal with groups of people.

What is true of one English, Jewish, Catholic, or Black person is not necessarily true of all—or even most—of them. We must avoid stereotyping people and, in the same vein, making the same kind of thinking error about other matters in which some is true (some Italians are short and dark) but not all is true (some Italians are tall, blonde, and blue-eyed).

This "some true/all implied" error is close to the "selected instances" error discussed above, in which generalizations are made on the basis of limited and unrepresentative sampling. The difference is that in the selected instances situation, one chooses selectively from among a variety of examples to use to build an argument; in the "some true/all implied" case, one just assumes, incorrectly, that what applies to some members of a group applies to all members.

### Imperfect Analogy

An analogy is a statement that suggests two things are similar in some important manner. Technically, the term we use for strong analogies is *metaphor* (e.g., the body is a machine); for weak analogies, the term is *simile* (e.g., the body is like a machine). In poetry, metaphors and similes cause no trouble, because we look upon poetry as essentially expressive. In research, metaphors and similes, and analogies in general, can be dangerous because they are often improperly applied. (See Chapter 7 for a discussion of metaphors and similes.)

For example, in earlier periods, kings argued that royal rule was natural by suggesting that the state (i.e., a nation or a country) is like a body and needs one heart or brain. Most modern thinkers argue that this is a false analogy; nations do not function like bodies. This analogy is spurious—created to justify the rule of kings. In the same way it can be said that, in certain respects, the human body is like a machine; but this resemblance is forced—it doesn't pay enough attention to all the ways in which the body is not like a machine.

It is perfectly acceptable to make analogies, but it is important to make sure that you do not use analogies incorrectly by comparing things that are too dissimilar or overextend reasonable analogies. When you want to use an analogy, make certain the analogy fits.

### Pushing Arguments to Absurd Extremes

Sometimes people push arguments to such extremes that they become patently ridiculous. We might do this in trying to attack notions that are contrary to ours; in some cases, we unwittingly push our arguments too far. For example, consider the famous "camel's nose" argument. You must be careful when dealing with a camel, the argument goes, not to let him poke his nose into your tent, because once he pokes his nose in, the rest of the camel will soon follow. Implicit in this argument is that once a certain thing happens, you cannot limit what else will happen. (This is also known as the "slippery slope" argument.)

You must be careful that you don't take some notion you have, which may be valid, and extend it so far (and generalize about it so much) that you lose credibility.

## Misrepresenting Ideas

The misrepresentation of another person's ideas comes about, usually, through carelessness and inattention. Many researchers make these kinds of slips, which can lead to very serious errors in their conclusions. You must be careful that the material you use accurately reflects a writer's ideas. For example, an author may say something rather general in one paragraph and qualify it in the next. If you do not include the qualification when discussing the work, you may be misrepresenting and distorting the writer's thoughts.

For example, suppose that a folklorist writes, "Polish jokes make one basic point—Poles are stupid, dirty, disgusting people. This is quite absurd, obviously." If you were to quote this passage but leave out the second sentence, you would be distorting the author's ideas. And if you were to quote only the phrase "Poles are stupid, dirty, disgusting people," you would be distorting his or her ideas even more. Sometimes leaving just one word out of a quote (such as *not* or *no*) can result in a major distortion and misrepresentation.

You must be careful to represent any writer you quote correctly. When you use quoted material, it is a good idea to double-check it, to be certain you have quoted the person accurately, and not left out a letter or a line (which sometimes happens). That is why it is a good idea to keep photocopies of the original pages from any material you will be quoting.

## Means Between Extremes

In the United States we believe in compromises—agreements between contending parties in which each gives up something to reach a solution to some impasse. This notion that the midpoint between extremes is correct or acceptable does not work in the area of logic and right reasoning, and can lead to absurd situations. For example, suppose a dictator in a certain country decides to kill all the old maids and bachelors. His wife argues that this is crazy, and he shouldn't kill any of the old maids and bachelors. If he were to decide to compromise and kill only half of the old maids and bachelors, would that mean his position is a reasonable one? Obviously not. Sometimes an extreme position (don't kill any old maids or bachelors) can be correct and a "moderate" position (kill only half of the old maids and bachelors) can be absurd.

We should examine ideas in terms of their merits and of their consequences, not in terms of whether they occupy a position between two so-called extremes or what seem to be extremes.

## A Final Note

In recent years a branch of informal logic known as *critical thinking* has become very popular, and many universities now offer courses in critical thinking. There are also a wide variety of textbooks on this subject. Those who are interested in this subject and wish to pursue it further are advised to take a relevant course and/or to purchase one of the many textbooks available.

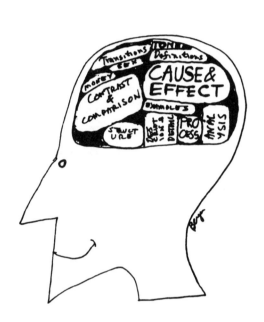

Exposition is writing that explains. In general, it answers the questions how? and why? If we go into any university library, most of the books we find on the shelves are examples of exposition. Philosophies, histories, literary essays, theories of economics, studies of government and law, the findings of sociology, the investigations of science—all these, however different, have for their purpose to explain. Although exposition often is formal and academic, it appears also in magazines and newspapers, in any place where people look for explanations. It is the most common kind of writing, the sort with which we conduct our workaday affairs—the business letter, the doctor's case study, the lawyer's brief, the engineer's report—and the writing with which we attempt to control our world.

Thomas S. Kane and Leonard J. Peters, **Writing Prose: Techniques and Purposes** (1986, p. 169)

# Chapter 17

## Writing a Research Report

**Good Secret Agents Don't
Keep Everything Secret**

Throughout this book I have used the metaphor of the researcher as a detective or secret agent, trying to find certain kinds of information. Once you find the information you are looking for, you must tell someone what you've found—otherwise that information cannot be used. To communicate what you have found, you will usually need to write a report. There is a fairly standard way of writing up one's research, based on logic and the way our minds work.

Reports give researchers an opportunity to present their findings and to discuss the results of their research. The purpose of the research report is to offer a clear and unambiguous statement of what was done, how it was done, and what was found. The following sections discuss the specifics of how to accomplish this.

**The Format of the Research Paper**

There is a standard format for research papers; this includes an introduction and sections on methods, findings, and discussion. Each is discussed in turn below.

*Introduction.* The introduction is a discussion of the problem or subject being studied. It should offer readers a sense of context and tell them what was being investigated—the topic, the research question, the researcher's original hypothesis, or whatever. Background is also presented in this section, including information about previous research on the subject. The introduction should provide readers with an overview and situate the research project in a larger context.

*Methods.* This section details the methods used in the study and explains why they were used. Discussion of the researcher's choice of methods is crucial, because every methodology has certain strong points and deficiencies.

*Findings.* This section presents the data—numerical or otherwise—collected in the course of the research. In the case of the content analysis of newspaper comic strips, for instance, the findings section would include a table displaying the numerical data to be analyzed. In the case of depth interviews, the researcher might offer representative quotations from respondents in this section. The researcher should always try to find appropriate ways of presenting the data and findings; often these include tables, figures, charts, and quotations—all of which allow readers to see for themselves what the researcher found. The important thing here is "Show, don't tell." The findings section should also include a discussion of the data analysis and the researcher's explanation of the data's significance. That is, the researcher must interpret his or her findings for readers in ways they can understand.

*Conclusions and summary.* This final section is devoted to the conclusions the researcher has reached based on his or her findings, as well as to discussion of such matters as problems the researcher faced in conducting the study, how the research relates to research on the same or similar topics done by others, the implications of the research for the social and political order, and how the research suggests other studies that might be pursued.

The format of the research paper is designed to shed as much light as possible on how the research was conducted. It is assumed that the researcher is an ethical person who is impartial and is trying to find accurate information. Sometimes researchers conduct studies to test hypotheses (guesses about something); in other cases, they want to get more information about particular topics or problems. In all cases, however, researchers have a moral obligation to be as honest as possible and to present their findings as accurately as they can. They also must respect the privacy and dignity of any informants who participate in their research projects.

## The Style of the Research Report

A research report should be written in a formal style, one appropriate to scholarly work. As I mentioned in Chapter 14, formal style in the past generally included the writer's referring to him- or herself only in the third person ("the researcher found") or in the first person plural ("we found"); now, many style authorities see nothing wrong with an author's using the first person singular ("I found"). In formal writing, however, you should take care to avoid a loose, conversational style that is inappropriate. Some people seem to equate a highly formal, stilted style with scholarly work, but it is the quality of the thinking and research that is most important.

A research report should be written in a gender-neutral manner. One way to do so and still avoid having to write "he or she" and "his or her" repeatedly is to use plural pronouns where possible.

Avoid jargon as much as you can. When you use a technical term or an unusual term, define it, so your reader is clear about how you are using it. In some cases, of course, when you are dealing with highly technical matters, it is impossible to write in plain English. You have to judge the fit between your use of jargon or technical terms and your readers.

If you use the first person in your report, you should write in the active voice as much as possible (e.g., "I interviewed three subjects"). If you want to avoid the first person as well as the stilted sound of the third person, you will find the passive voice useful (e.g., "Three subjects were interviewed" instead of "I interviewed three subjects" or "The researcher interviewed three subjects").

Reports are conventionally typed or word processed, using double-spacing with a flush left margin and (for ease of reading) a ragged right margin. Most word processors can easily justify the right-hand margin, but this often leads to wide gaps between words.

## Using Quotations and Paraphrases

There is a simple way to avoid accidental plagiarism: If you use words written by others, give those authors credit. You do this by making it clear that you have used their words. Quotations are useful as a form of "evidence" to show particular things; also, they sometimes express what we want to say in particularly appropriate and distinctive ways.

*Quotes of fewer than 40 words.* If you are quoting someone and the quote has fewer than 40 words (approximately three lines), the convention is to put quote marks around the material and integrate the quoted material into a sentence. It is a good idea to identify, briefly, the person being quoted. For example:

In *Beyond Laughter,* Martin Grotjahn (1966), a Freudian psychoanalyst, says the relationship between comedy and the subconscious is simple, because "the tragic guilt of the son is displaced upon the father. In comedy it is the father who is guilty" (p. 86). What he means here is that there is a switch in roles and it is the son who ends up playing the role of the father.

*Quotes of more than 40 words.* With longer quotes, the convention is to indent five spaces from the place where paragraphs begin, have a flush left margin, and not use quote marks at the beginning or end. This is called a block quote, or an extract. An example follows:

In *Beyond Laughter,* Martin Grotjahn (1966), a Freudian psychoanalyst, discusses the relationship that exists between the subconscious and comedy. He writes:

> The thesis is simple, straightforward, and convincing: the tragic guilt of the son is displaced upon the father. In comedy it is the father who is guilty. This inversion of guilt can be seen in Shakespeare's classic comedies as in all others. The villain is the victim of his own villainy. (p. 86)

What Grotjahn means by this is that comedy is connected, in an inverse manner, to the Oedipus complex, which would explain why comedy is both universal and so important to people.

If you use a long quotation, it should be because you believe the quote has substantial importance for the argument you are developing, and you should point out why you have used the quote and why it is significant.

*Paraphrasing.* We paraphrase when we want to summarize some-one else's ideas but don't feel it is necessary to quote him or her. If you decide to paraphrase a statement or idea of another author, be careful that you don't inadvertently use his or her exact language.

Grotjahn (1966) believes that comedy involves an inversion in which guilt is displaced from sons to their fathers. This explains . . . .

The *Publication Manual of the American Psychological Association* (fourth edition, 1994) discusses quotations and author citations in considerable detail. In APA style, footnotes are not used to supply information about quoted or cited material. Instead, the name of the author and the date of the publication (and page number in the case of a quote) are included in parentheses in the text; the full bibliographic information on cited works appears in a reference section at the end of the paper or book. Generally, APA rules for placement of reference citations are as follows:

- *In midsentence:* End the passage with quotation marks, cite the source in parentheses immediately after the quotation marks, and continue the sentence.
- *At the end of a sentence:* Close the quoted passage with quotation marks, cite the source in parentheses immediately after the quotation marks, and end with the period or other punctuation outside the final parenthesis.
- *At the end of a block quote:* Cite the quoted source in parentheses after the final punctuation mark.

In some styles it is acceptable to put citations elsewhere—for example, before a block quote. The important thing is to be consistent in whatever style you use. If APA style is required for the work, follow that manual's guidelines.

## Reference Lists

In APA and some other styles, in-text citations are all keyed to a list of references that is included at the end of the report. Such a reference list should include only those sources used in the research project and cited in the report, unlike a bibliography, which may also include works that are useful for background reading.

Every work cited in the report must appear in the reference list, and every work listed in the references must be cited in the report. The entries in the reference list should contain all or some of the following elements (depending on the type of work and the reference style followed):

- author name(s)
- date of publication
- title of the article or book
- for articles, the name of the periodical in which the article was published, as well as volume number (and sometimes the issue number) and the article's inclusive page numbers
- for books, the city where the book was published
- for books, the name of the publisher

Creating a reference list and citing works in text correctly can be very complicated. If your instructor wishes you to follow a particular style, you should consult whatever list of guidelines is available for that style and follow it carefully.

## Numbers

There are several standard ways to present numbers in text. The general rule in APA style is to use words for (that is, write out) numbers less than 10 and numerals for numbers 10 and higher, though there are exceptions. For example, numerals are always used for certain kinds of measurements and to represent time, and in tables, all numbers appear as numerals. When used in direct comparison with larger numbers, numbers under 10 should appear as numerals ("3 out of 25 subjects").

Numerals cannot be used to start sentences; often it is best to rewrite a sentence to avoid the problem of writing out large numbers. For example, instead of saying "Thirty-seven out of 42 respondents gave . . . ," you can say "Out of 42 respondents, 37 gave . . . ."

## Concluding Your Research Report

You should end your research paper with some kind of a concluding statement. There are two common ways to do this. The first is to write a brief summary in which you recapitulate your findings and discuss their significance. This is a way of wrapping things up and reminding your reader of what you have done and what you have found. The second is to summarize what you've done and use your findings to arrive at some new insight—a generalization, an idea, a theory—that stems from your research and that may have implications for further research.

The length of your conclusion will be relative to the length and complexity of your research project. For the projects discussed in this book, conclusions of two or three paragraphs may be sufficient. For longer research projects, which may be quite complex, you will generally need more space to conclude your report.

You may wish to use a "cue" or "signal word"—such as *finally* or *in conclusion*—to indicate that you are concluding your argument. In some cases, you may be able to bring your argument full circle and return to some word or idea you mentioned in the beginning of the paper and the problem being discussed. Or you may find some kind of witty remark or clever wordplay that is appropriate. Whatever the case, you must find some manner of ending the paper that will satisfy your reader. A paper should come to a conclusion, not just stop because you've reached the minimum number of words required.

# References

American Psychological Association. (1994). *Publication manual of the American Psychological Association* (4th ed.). Washington, DC: Author.

Aristotle. (1941). *The basic works of Aristotle* (R. McKeon, Ed. and Trans.). New York: Random House.

Baudrillard, J. (1988). *America*. London: Verso.

Berger, A. A. (1984). *Signs in contemporary culture: An introduction to semiotics*. New York: Annenberg-Longman.

Berger, A. A. (1990). *Scripts: Writing for radio and television*. Newbury Park, CA: Sage.

Berger, P. L., & Berger, B. (1972). *Sociology: A biographical approach*. New York: Basic Books.

Berkhofer, R. E., Jr. (1969). *A behavioral approach to historical analysis*. New York: Free Press.

Bogart, L. (1985). *Polls and the awareness of public opinion* (2nd ed.). New Brunswick, NJ: Transaction.

Brewer, J., & Hunter, A. (1989). *Multimethod research: A synthesis of styles*. Newbury Park, CA: Sage.

Durkheim, E. (1965). *The elementary forms of the religious life* (J. W. Swain, Trans.). New York: Free Press.

Fairchild, H. P. (1967). *Dictionary of sociology and related sciences (your college course at a glance)*. Totowa, NJ: Littlefield, Adams.

Grotjahn, M. (1966). *Beyond laughter*. New York: McGraw-Hill.

Hayakawa, S. I., in collaboration with Berger, A. A., & Chandler, A. (1978). *Language in thought and action* (4th ed.). New York: Harcourt Brace Jovanovich.

Kane, T. S., & Peters, L. J. (1986). *Writing prose: Techniques and purposes* (6th ed.). New York: Oxford University Press.

Kern, M. (1989). *30-second politics: Political advertising in the eighties*. New York: Praeger.

Komidar, J. S. (1952). The uses of the library. In W. J. Goode & P. K. Hatt (Eds.), *Methods in social research*. New York: McGraw-Hill.

Lakoff, G., & Johnson, M. (1980). *Metaphors we live by*. Chicago: University of Chicago Press.

Leon, R. L. (1988). *Psychiatric interviewing: A primer*. New York: Elsevier.

Lipset, S. M. (1968). Some methodological considerations. In S. M. Lipset & R. Hofstadter (Eds.), *Sociology and history: Methods*. New York: Basic Books.

Lowery, S., & DeFleur, M. L. (1983). *Milestones in mass communication research: Media effects*. New York: Longman.

Milgram, S. (1965). Liberating effects of group pressure. *Journal of Personality and Social Psychology, 1*, 127-134.

Moss, A., & Holder, C. (1988). *Improving student writing: A guidebook for faculty in all disciplines*. Pomona: California State Polytechnic University.

Progoff, I. (1975). *At a journal workshop: The basic text and guide for using the intensive journal*. New York: Dialogue House Library.

Root, R. L., Jr. (1987). *The rhetorics of popular culture: Advertising, advocacy, and entertainment*. Westport, CT: Greenwood.

Rubin, R. B., Rubin, A. M., & Piele, L. J. (1990). *Communication research: Strategies and sources* (2nd ed.). Belmont, CA: Wadsworth.

Saussure, F. de. (1966). *A course in general linguistics* (W. Baskin, Trans.). New York: McGraw-Hill.

Schellenberg, J. A. (1974). *An introduction to social psychology* (2nd ed.). New York: Random House.

Schwartz, T. (1974). *The responsive chord*. Garden City, NY: Doubleday.

Simon, J. L. (1969). *Basic research methods in social science: The art of empirical investigation*. New York: Random House.

Sjoberg, G., & Nett, R. (1968). *A methodology for social research*. New York: Harper & Row.

Spradley, J. P. (1979). *The ethnographic interview*. New York: Holt, Rinehart & Winston.

Tosuner-Fikes, L. (1982). A guide to anthropological fieldwork on contemporary American culture. In C. P. Kottak (Ed.), *Researching American culture*. Ann Arbor: University of Michigan Press.

Turner, R. (1968). Role: Sociological aspects. In *International encyclopedia of the social sciences* (Vol. 13). New York: Macmillan.

Ward, J., & Hansen, K. A. (1987). *Search strategies in mass communication*. New York: Longman.

Warnick, B., & Inch, E. S. (1989). *Critical thinking and communication: The use of reason in argument*. New York: Macmillan.

Wimmer, R. D., & Dominick, J. R. (1983). *Mass media research: An introduction*. Belmont, CA: Wadsworth.

Wright, C. R. (1986). *Mass communication: A sociological perspective* (3rd ed.). New York: Random House.

Zinsser, W. (1976). *On writing well* (3rd ed.). New York: Harper & Row.

Zito, G. V. (1975). *Methodology and meanings: Varieties of sociological inquiry*. New York: Praeger.

# Name Index

# Subject Index

# About the Author

DECODER
MAN

**Arthur Asa Berger** is Professor of Broadcast and Electronic Communication Arts at San Francisco State University, where he has taught since 1965. He took early retirement in January 1998 and now teaches only during the fall semesters. He has published more than 100 articles, numerous book reviews, and more than 30 books. Among his latest books are *Essentials of Mass Communication Theory* (1995), *Bloom's Morning: Coffee, Comforters and the Hidden Meaning of Everyday Life* (1997), *The Genius of the Jewish Joke* (1997), *Narratives in Popular Culture, Media, and Everyday Life* (1997), *The Art of Comedy Writing* (1997), and a comic murder mystery about postmodernism, *Postmortem for a Postmodernist* (1997). A companion reader to this mystery, titled *The Postmodern Presence: Readings on Postmodernism in American Culture and Society*, is currently in press. He is now working on two other mysteries: *The Hamlet Case*, which deals with different ways of interpreting Shakespeare's *Hamlet*, and *Murder ad Hominem*, which shows how print advertisements and radio and TV commercials can be analyzed from the perspectives of multiple disciplines.

Dr. Berger is married, has two children, and lives in Mill Valley, California. He has a page on the Internet that includes a list of his books and a number of his articles; his e-mail address is aberger@sfsu.edu.